"I can say unequivocally, this book should be on every manager's and HR specialist's desk."

Ada M. Tuck, Corporate Management Consultant, Human Resources, Government of Canada

"This book should be on the desk of every HR manager in Canada."

Kate Porter, President Porter Studio Ltd. & lecturer Simon Fraser University

"I read your book and I think it is brilliant. We will purchase 50 books."

Arlette Watwood, Human Resources Corporate Services, City of Calgary Fire Department

"Managing Human Rights at Work is an incredibly useful day-to-day tool. When I'm in a dilemma I go to the book thinking 'what does Stephen have to say about this?' On each occasion Stephen's advice has been invaluable."

Carmen Grant, Director of Human Resources, Purdy's Chocolates Ltd.

"This book is an invaluable resource for Managers, Supervisors and Human Resources professionals. We bought a supply for all of our Managers and Supervisors."

Marian L. Exmann, Associate Vice President, Employee Relations, Douglas College

"Every supervisor, manager and company executive today would do well to read it and keep the principles in mind."

Dave Crisp, speaker on effectiveness and ethics, former Senior Vice President, Human Resources, Hudson's Bay Company

"Stephen's book is applicable for anyone who supervises employees or interacts with others in the workplace. This book opened my eyes in a very positive way."

Ellen Retelle, B.S., M. Ed., Ph.D. Professor of Education, University of Lethbridge

"If people take the time to read your book, they can avoid 70% of their human rights problems."

Michael Heitmann, CKJS radio Winnipeg

"Your book makes it comfortable and easy to understand for someone who may be unfamiliar with human rights law. It reminds me of the book The Wealthy Barber and what it did to help people understand financial planning and investment in Canada."

Dr. Palaniappan Andiappan, Professor, Management and Labour Studies, Odette School of Business, University of Windsor

"Highly readable and filled with practical tips for business, it touches on many hot-button issues that many supervisors, managers and employees aren't aware of."

Mike Dempster, Business Edge magazine

"This book is well worth the read. Everyone in the workplace should read this book."

Geoff Currier, Broadcaster CJOB radio, Winnipeg

"A great read for anyone. Fantastic read."

Erin Isfeld, Broadcaster A-Channel Winnipeg

"The book is full of great stories. We could talk all day."

Dave Kelly, Broadcaster A-Channel, Calgary

"This book is a 'must read' for anyone who wants to get a better grip on this complicated subject matter. I highly recommend it."

Fanny Kiefer, Radio and Television Broadcaster & Host of Shaw TV's Studio 4

"His book is chock-a-block with practical tips and stories. Some of them are hair-raising."

Don Hill, Broadcaster of Alberta's Wild Rose Forum CBC Radio, Edmonton

"I think what people will find interesting about the book is that they are very straight forward, small, readable tips."

Jeff Rogstad, Broadcaster, CFQC CTV Saskatoon

Managing Human Rights At Work

101 practical tips to prevent
human rights disasters

by Stephen Hammond

Harassment Solutions Inc./Vancouver

Editing by Pam Withers
Proofreading by Susan Gordon and Angelina Gordon
Cover design by Dale Costanzo
Layout by Ted Schredd
Back cover photo by Ales Piro

Printed and bound in Canada by Friesens Corporation
Fifth printing 2009

National Library of Canada Cataloguing in Publication

Hammond, Stephen, 1959-
    Managing human rights at work : 101 practical tips to
prevent human rights disasters / Stephen Hammond.

Includes bibliographical references.
ISBN 978-0-9734954-0-9

    1. Diversity in the workplace--Canada. 2. Employee rights--
Canada. 3. Organizational justice--Canada. I. Title.

HF5549.5.E428H34 2004   658.3'008   C2004-901362-9

*This book is dedicated to my parents,
Bob & Gerrie Hammond.
They gave me their values and told
me I could do anything.*

Contents

Chapter Four - Treating "Different" People Differently...61

Chapter Five - Inclusiveness, Not Affirmative Action.....76

Chapter Six - Management Needs To Know.................94

About the Author

Stephen Hammond is a consultant, speaker, and trainer in the field of workplace human rights. Since 1992 Stephen has rescued organizations from human rights disasters and enhanced businesses by encouraging them to change with the times. While Stephen is a lawyer by trade and still a member of the Law Society of British Columbia, he no longer practices law. He holds a professional designation with the Canadian Association of Professional Speakers and Stephen's goal is to support welcoming workplaces.

At a relatively young age, Stephen's life experiences shaped his views and passions regarding human rights. Between obtaining a Bachelor of Arts degree from the University of Manitoba and a Bachelor of Laws degree from Osgoode Hall Law School, Stephen was the executive director of one of Manitoba's political parties and was thrown into jail in communist Poland, accused of being a spy for the West. Stephen was called to the Bar in British Columbia in 1988 and proceeded to work in the field of labour and employee relations both in the private and public sectors.

Stephen regularly appears on radio and television programs to discuss harassment and human rights issues. He doesn't shy away from issues just because they are sensationally reported or misunderstood. Instead, Stephen tries to get to the heart of complex and often difficult cases.

Born in Winnipeg, Manitoba, Stephen has called Vancouver, British Columbia home since 1990. His volunteer time has included Big Brothers, the Western Institute for the Deaf and Hard of Hearing, the Clean Air Coalition, Amnesty International, as well as local associations devoted to protecting and enhancing communities. In his spare time, Stephen is on the steep and deep slopes in the winter, while in the summer he makes futile attempts to get a decent handicap on British Columbia's beautiful golf courses.

Acknowledgements

When I first met Jack Boomer and he found out what I did for a living, he told me to write a book. Then, when I joined the Vancouver chapter of the Canadian Association of Professional Speakers, speaker after speaker told me the same thing: Write a book. Without the combination of Jack and CAPS, this book would not have been written. I owe my gratitude to Jack Boomer and all those speakers, close to home and far away.

When I asked for opinions and critical comments, I got it. To my Fasttrackers, Pat Allen, Bill Carpenter, Rosemary Dunne, Joni Mar and Stan Tonoski, thanks for your valuable feedback. Pat, your comments didn't scare me. Joni, yours did. However I slogged through each and every comment and this book is much better even though I cursed you with each change.

I also received great feedback and information from Pippa Blake, Maureen Fitzgerald, Susan Gordon, Gary Hall, Pat Hardin, Rajpal Kohli, Sherri Newcomen, Robie Scholefield, Sandra Sundhu, Penny Goldrick, Susan Rae, Don Meen, Rosemary Sadlier, and Colleen Trounce. Thank you all.

To the 62 people who helped me with the title, thank you. William Hann, Rene Lash, and Erwin Nest gave me the combination of words that led to the final title, so they received the prize.

When I asked Pam Withers to edit my book, I was worried about losing my voice and it never happened. This book is so much better because of her guidance and advice. My layout and all-round funny guy, Ted Schredd, kept on coming up with suggestions when I least wanted to hear them - right near the end. Thankfully, I had just enough common sense left to accede to most of his suggestions, even if it meant giving up a day on the slopes. And without my proofers, Angelina Gordon and Susan Gordon, you'd be stumbling through all kinds of mistakes. Thanks for your watchful eyes. Any errors or omissions, I take full responsibility.

Introduction

Managing the workplace is tough. Countless things can go wrong and people, unlike machines, are prone to say the wrong thing or have their words misinterpreted. However, when it comes to issues of human rights-characteristics such as sex and race that we can't change, or religion and marital status that we aren't expected to change-you may find yourself with a disaster on your hands. If you have a bad day and yell at someone, you can always correct that. An apology will go a long way. However, make a disparaging comment about a person's nationality, skin colour, sex, or religion, and it may take a lot more than an apology to get that person back to respecting you and your working relationship. That's because basic human rights, even the simple comments at work, go to the core of each one of us. When employees and managers cross over that line, whether in a subtle or in-your-face manner, staff loyalty takes a dive. At best, you might continue to employ distressed employees, but at worst, they will bolt the first chance they get. And often they talk, usually quietly, sometimes loudly, to friends and acquaintances.

This book is designed to help you, the manager and supervisor, manage the human rights process a little more easily.

1

This book has no intention of making people more progressive or liberal in their attitudes. It is not designed to convince leaders to change the way they think. It is designed to help those who are in the tricky art of managing people and workplaces in understanding human rights issues and preventing human rights disasters. *Yeah, right*, I can hear some of you thinking. *This book is about political correctness, which is total B.S.* Think whatever you want, but don't ignore the message just because you disagree with it. In other words, don't shoot the messenger. I give you this free advice: Hear me out now, or pay other lawyers and specialists to get you out of trouble later. I want to help you avoid the mistakes that can get your rear caught in the human rights grinder. Look at each chapter and decide if your workplace is in line with the issues it covers: the laws, tribunal or court decisions, and overall logic. If you, as a savvy manager handle human rights issues *before* they become a problem, or deal with them at the first sign of trouble, it doesn't matter whether you yourself subscribe to so-called political correctness. Just know this: Ignoring human rights problems at work can land you in hot water, can bring a case against you either through the human rights process or the courts. When that happens, win or lose, you're wasting valuable time and resources dealing with public relations and plummeting workplace morale.

Then again, *not* suffering bad P.R. or a human rights case is no guarantee that all is well. Many an employee who feels discriminated against is loathe to file a complaint, but the result is nearly as deadly: high turnover, low productivity, a tainted reputation in the talent pool, and a snowball's chance in hell of securing an employer-of-choice designation. It doesn't matter whether you have two or 2,000 employees.

Do you have the right to run your business as you want? Yes...to a point. In Canada, employees, customers, and individuals get basic human rights protection from provincial, territorial and federal human rights legislation. How important are these pieces of law? Human rights legislation is often referred to as quasi-constitutional, which means that if any piece of legislation comes into conflict with human rights legislation, the human rights law will prevail. Even if a province or other jurisdiction appears to have watered down human rights legislation, don't be fooled; rights are protected by equality provisions in the constitution's Charter of Rights and Freedoms.

Some people say the human rights and the legal pendulums have swung too far. They believe it's poised to swing back, and this will give them a break. Not only do I see no indication of a reversal; I see plenty of signs that our courts and tribunals will push the pendulum further and further towards supporting individuals seeking to assert their human rights. The courts, through our constitution's Charter of Rights and Freedoms, are trumpeting a clear and consistent message: *If you do harm, you will pay.* While the message might not always be obvious from a criminal law perspective, it is becoming more obvious from a civil and human rights perspective. Who'd have thought that an entire religious diocese could cease to exist paying for past abuses? Who envisioned that a new-age human rights principle of pay equity would end up costing businesses and governments millions and billions of dollars in back pay?

Such cases have occurred and will continue occurring until the courts and tribunals believe Canada has achieved better equality of opportunity and results. For better or for worse, the businesses that come to grips with this, and start adjusting work practices and client procedures accordingly, will thrive. Sometimes the results aren't tangible, unless compared to a business competitor who has attracted banner headlines for putting his foot in his mouth or for paying a judgement award for not keeping up with the times. Suddenly, business positives are defined as an ability to keep one's eyes on the bottom line instead of being sucked into the vortex of a human rights complaint.

In the book I have given you 101 tips. I've tried my best to lay out the tips prior to the point I want you to get.

Some of the tips are straightforward and others are more complex. I've tried my best to keep the legalese out of the process, but we can't avoid the law. I think it's easy to say the law drives the human rights process because there are so many commissions, tribunals, and courts that give us guidance and sometimes harsh words. However, what really drives this process is the Canadian sensibility, which says that respecting and upholding basic human rights is a major part of what makes us one of the most desirable places to live. When a workplace is missing that sensibility, it's rarely a place where people want to stay or clients want to support.

Don't skip Chapter 2: *Are you Accommodating?* This growing area of judge-made human rights law may be perplexing, frustrating, and ever-evolving, but for the sake of your business, you want to get some kind of grip on it. It continues to perplex scholars, lawyers, judges, managers and human rights practitioners, yet I hope I've laid it out in a way that will help you better understand it, thereby helping your business.

In most examples, I use the real names and real cases available to the public (unless I gathered additional information from an interview). This approach is not meant to hurt anyone. Most people are trying their best - even if they end up with disastrous consequences. I thought about using fictitious examples, but I realized it wouldn't work. You need to hear about real examples and learn from real mistakes.

Throughout this book I make reference to "business." If your business is a private company - big or small, subject to free market forces or not - this book applies to you. If you work for the government, a quasi-public body, or a non-profit organization, this book also applies to you. Why? Because your "business" involves meeting goals within a defined budget. There's advice here for your internal business (dealing with employees), as well as for your external business (dealing with customers and clients). Just as human rights legislation applies to all workplaces - private, public and non-profit - so does this book.

4

"In my youth, there were words you couldn't say in front of a girl; now you can't say 'girl.'"

Tom Lehrer

1

The Word Game

Chinaman Lake lies just outside Hudson's Hope in northern British Columbia. It was named a long time ago. But times change, and what was innocuous for decades can come around and bite people on their behinds. In October 1996, Victor Wong, president of the Vancouver Association of Chinese-Canadians, petitioned the province to change the name. Not only did the government agree; it also decided to rescind the names of Chinamen Flat, Chinamen Rapids and Chinaman Flat Rapids in other parts of the province. When the news got out, many people (mostly non-Chinese) were outraged. "Political correctness run amok," people cried. Hundreds of miles away, Vancouver newspapers ran letters from people who asked, "What's next? Change the name of English Bay?" Even some Chinese Canadians voiced displeasure at having to deal with negative publicity arising from the controversy.

Today, citizens of B.C. can still find references to these names, but officially, they no longer adorn the lake, rapids and other points of geography.

Tip #1 Listen to the words people use

Not long ago, during a session I was leading about workplace harassment, someone raised the issue of Chinamen Lake, offering it as an example of how political correctness had gone too far, and how we waste time and tax dollars on issues insignificant to most people. The group comprised well-paid, reasonably well educated white males, with a few exceptions. As I made stumbling efforts at convincing the group that Chinaman was a derogatory word for Chinese people, a Chinese Canadian employee raised his hand. This in itself was remarkable, since I've long noticed that employees of male-dominated workplaces avoid revealing weaknesses. But this brave soul had a message. He said, "Whenever I hear the word 'chinaman,' it reminds me of the times in the schoolyard when I was on the ground and someone was kicking me in the head." I knew we had a teachable moment. You could have heard a pin drop.

Words have an impact in any line of work. Mere words can bring down morale, make valuable people quit their jobs, and lose customers on the spot. We all know that racial and sexual slurs are no longer tolerated at work. Today's debate is about how far such sensitivity goes. Confusion and uncertainty reign.

Take, for example, the word "black" to describe African Americans. Years ago, I asked an African American friend from the States, "So what's the big deal with calling black people black?" He told me to look up the words "black" and "white" in the dictionary, then we'd talk. Here are direct quotes from my Concise Oxford dictionary:

White

- The colour of milk, fresh snow, common salt or a swan's plumage.
- Innocent, unstained, of harmless kind.
- White-haired or white-headed boy, highly favoured person.

- White hands, innocent or integrity.
- White hope, person who is expected to attain renown.
- White man, person of honourable character and good breeding.
- White war: war without bloodshed, economic warfare.
- White witch: uses power for beneficent purposes only.

Black

- Of hands, clothes dirty.
- Deadly, sinister, wicked, hateful (black-hearted; black ingratitude; not so black as one is painted, better than one's reputation).
- Dismal (black despair).
- Angry, sulky, threatening (black looks).
- Implying disgrace or condemnation.
- Presenting tragedy or bitter reality in comic terms (black comedy, humour, joke).
- Of goods, etc.: not to be handled by workers on strike.
- Contravening economic regulations (black market).
- In person's black books: out of favour with him.
- Blacklist (of persons under suspicion, liable to punishment or unfavourable treatment, etc.).
- Black mail: compel, compulsion, to make payment or action in return for concealment of discreditable secrets, etc.
- Black mark (of discredit against one's name).
- Black spot, place of danger or difficulty, esp. area with high accident rate, etc.

I got the point. While there are exceptions to the definitions noted above, most people typically use "white" in positive terms and "black" in negative terms. Since that's not going to change for a long while, some African American leaders decided it is better to use language that

7

identifies people by heritage rather than by skin colour. White and Black people still use "Black" to describe African Americans, and no one thinks that's a crime, but the above list illuminates why some terms are preferable to others, and why some can make people uncomfortable.

In Canada, both Black Canadian and African Canadian seem to be acceptable terms. There is still going to be confusion about the use of certain

> Why use terms that make some feel comfortable and others uncomfortable?

words and inconsistencies in our language, hence we may find ourselves in a quandary. Language is constantly changing, however if we are respectful with our terminology, most people will understand if we are willing to learn or make mistakes.

Tip #2 Adapt terminology to suit your audience

In Canada, confusion reigns over what to call those who were here before European settlers. Most people are aware that Christopher Columbus named them "Indians" because he was looking for India when he stumbled across North America. I heard one Canadian aboriginal leader say, "Thank goodness Columbus wasn't looking for Turkey."

"So, what's the latest term I'm supposed to use?!" people ask in frustration. Or, "You can't say anything without offending someone." What *is* a person to do?

The most common terms are Indian, Native, Aboriginal and First Nations. I say "Aboriginal" when I'm speaking about, or to, aboriginal people. But I also listen to the terms they use. If I hear someone use "Indian", I use "Indian". If a person says "First Nations", I use that term. It's no skin off my nose to adapt to a situation. In fact it's often about having social graces. If Robert likes to be called Bob, and Marnie likes to be called Marnie Jane, I have no trouble adapting, either.

Then there's the aboriginal nickname "chief." Aboriginal men tell me they often get this label in the workplace, without ever having asked for it. Non-aboriginals tell me "chief" is supposed to be a compliment because it implies a community leader. Yet, how often are non-aboriginal men nicknamed "councilor," "mayor," "premier" or "prime minister"?

Is it not odd that so many Aboriginal men get this nickname when others do not? Aboriginal leaders tell me, "Don't call a person 'chief' unless he or she is one."

Tip #3 Look to parallels for appropriate language

Then there's the gender challenge - above all, the use of the word "girl." While phrases like "you go girl!" and "girl power" create a positive image, overall, "girl" tends to be a negative in the workplace. "For that information, go see the girl at reception," some will say. Where a man is at the same reception desk, how likely would we say, "For that information, go see the boy at reception"? Perhaps only if it's "Bring Your Child to Work Day."

Sure, men and women will still use "girls night out" and "boys night out," or "the boys are getting together tonight" and "the girls are going to a movie this weekend." But when using words regarding gender, just consider the parallel. If you'd use "boy" for a man in the same way you'd use "girl" for a woman, you're usually safe. If not, refer to adult men as men and adult women as women.

Tip #4 Callous words will distract from your message

In recent years, the term guys, as in "you guys," is getting increasing usage for referring to either gender. And yet, the female parallel of "guys" is "gals." Ask yourself how many people would address a group of men and women, "See you gals later." If there is so much as one man in the group, you'll get laughter and comments, guaranteed. Using "guys" in a mixed group, might also grab some attention.

I was at a business association meeting where the presenter was a well-known and accomplished speaker. At one point, she referred to the audience as "you guys".

Having just written this piece, it caught my attention, but I didn't bother saying anything. However, after the break, this same speaker apologized to the group for calling us guys because one of the women had told her that she wasn't a guy. Is using "guys" a big deal? No, but those who continue to use gender-specific terms in mixed gender groups will find that some women take notice.

Is the business lesson here to never, ever say something that will offend others? Of course not. People can handle differences and even controversies, but they shouldn't have to put up with words that offend. Why let callous words get in the way of a message? If you've got something to say, draw attention to the substance, not to a lack of personal sensitivity.

Tip #5 Ditch outdated words

Of course, it's not enough to pay careful attention to your own vocabulary. As a supervisor, you're responsible for ensuring anyone connected to your business-employees, consultants-avoid language that can get your firm into trouble. You don't have to be the language police, but if a problem arises, take action. Worry less about a human rights commission than about the response of your staff.

Take, for example, the term "niggerhead," still used in some construction or maintenance workplaces to mean a boulder or object in the ground difficult to remove. Just because it has been used for eons with little objection does not mean a colleague won't take offence. Whether offence is meant or not, if you as a leader aspire to maximize employee output, commitment and retention, you've got to rid the workplace of words that offend.

Don't tell me we can't change our terminology. When I was a kid, we used to say, "eenie meanie, miney moe, catch a ..." Know what came next? I lived in a small town in Manitoba at the time, with no Black people around, and no one ever told me the word was wrong. Of course, it was wrong every time we used it, but I didn't know that. Today, kids say "eenie meanie miney moe, catch a tiger by the toe." Somewhere between my youth and the youth of today, we changed our terminology and it was for the better.

We also change our language when we grow up. I was born and partially raised in Winnipeg, where there was a relatively large Jewish population. Even in my rather w.a.s.p. neighbourhood of St. James, I rarely heard anyone say they were "jew'd" and when I did, I knew it was wrong. However, on my first move to Vancouver in the late 1970s, I regularly heard people use that term. I quickly figured out the Jewish population of Vancouver was quite small. As more Jews moved to Vancouver, I heard less and less terminology that would offend them.

Don't be afraid to say, "This is the year two thousand (and whatever), and it's time we stopped using words that are going to offend - regardless of how long we've used them."

Tip #6 Extreme examples won't trump common sense

Likewise, the buck stops at your desk when it comes to employees who justify their use of offensive language by pointing to cases where things have gone too far. In the early 1990s, Toronto Mayor June Rowlands barred the Barenaked Ladies from performing at city hall because the band's name "objectified women". The mayor was trying to protect women, but most people agree this was a strange way of going about it. The publicity that resulted helped the band go on to be a huge Canadian success.

Or, in January of 1999, David Howard, head of the Washington, D.C.'s District Office of Public Advocate, explained in a meeting that there would not be much money for the mayor's constituent services office. "I will have to be niggardly with this fund because it's not going to be a lot of money" he said. When he saw the shocked look on the faces of his colleagues, he realized they didn't understand that niggardly means stingy or miserly, and he tried to explain. But it was too late; people became furious over Mr. Howard's "racial slur."

11

Within days, he was pressured to offer his resignation to the mayor, and it was accepted. In early February, thanks partly to an international outcry, the mayor reinstated Howard, who nevertheless asked for a different job in the mayor's administration.

Back closer to home, I was working with a police department on issues of harassment in the workplace, when I got a call from a senior officer wanting advice about an incident involving a spokesperson who, at a gay and lesbian cultural event, talked to the media about the importance of reaching out to various communities. After the discussion, some women berated the spokesperson for using the term "lesbian," saying they preferred to be called "dykes". I assured the officer they were on safe ground using the word "lesbian" when referring to gay women. I've been in my field long enough to know when a request is overboard. If you are unsure, ask around before assuming you need to accommodate a request.

Language is always changing, and during changes, we often run into problems. Some will overreact, but that doesn't mean we throw new found sensitivities out the window. Smart leaders refuse to allow extreme or bizarre examples to be used as an excuse for continuing to allow employees to use offensive language.

Parting Tips for The Word Game

Tip #7 Keep up with changing language

Language is fluid; accept changes that make sense. If they don't make sense, feel free to seek out individuals who will explain. Develop a keen sense of observation and you'll soon acquire an ability to figure out the terms people prefer - by the terminology they use.

Tip #8 Correct mistakes and move on

If you do offend through disrespectful language, correct yourself, apologize if appropriate, and move on. Don't let one inappropriate word interfere with your message. Above all, don't say, "It's impossible to keep up with all the terminology." An offended person will take that to mean you are insensitive and it's only impossible when you're addressing individuals or groups you don't care about.

Tip #9 Correct employee language

If you hear employees or colleagues using inappropriate language, correct them. If you don't, and you are in a leadership role supervising employees, others will think you either agree with the language or you don't care. Be an ally to people who are subject to inappropriate language. Anyone "different" from the majority has to pick and choose battles to avoid being labeled a whiner. Fight some battles for them. You will get more productivity and loyalty that way. Besides, often the message is heard louder and more clearly when it comes from someone who doesn't appear to have a vested interest in the outcome.

"Reasonable people adapt themselves to the world. Unreasonable people attempt to adapt the world to themselves. All progress, therefore, depends on unreasonable people."

George Bernard Shaw

2

Are You Accommodating?

It is 1978 and you are the manager of a department within a large national department store. Since there are no Sunday openings at this time, your department earns its weekly profits between Thursday and Saturday evenings.

Theresa, a full-time employee since 1971, tells you on Tuesday that she will not be able to work her scheduled shift on Saturday, as she has joined the Seventh-Day Adventist Church. Seventh-Day Adventists strictly observe the Sabbath, which runs from sundown Friday to sundown Saturday.

Since all full-time employees know they must work three out of four Saturdays and two out of four Friday evenings per month, you figure it will come as no surprise to her when you downgrade her to part-time work on a contingency basis amounting to half the hours and considerably reduced benefits. You think you are being generous under the circumstances. After all, what would the other employees think if you were to make an exception for Theresa? Worse still, you'd be worried about other employees running off to join Theresa's church.

From a legal standing, you are not worried, because you know(remember, this is 1978) you are on solid ground. You didn't fire her because of her religion. You fired her because she couldn't work the hours she was hired to work and which other full-time employees work. So you are quite surprised when Theresa takes the store to the Human Rights Commission, claiming she has been discriminated against based on her religion. Still, you have no worries, because while it initially costs you a lot of your time, and later, costs your company considerable money, your decision is supported by the provincial Human Rights Board of Inquiry, the Divisional Court and the provincial Court of Appeal. You are thinking, "When will this woman give up? It's not even a good case."

Let's stop the suspense and fast forward to the case's finish. You lost at the Supreme Court of Canada, which ruled you had to accommodate Theresa. Over the years, the courts have used various wording and formulas, but as it stands, if you are going to discriminate against an employee or a customer based on a human rights ground, you better look at all the options to see if you can accommodate that person.

Yes, but what of employees who say, "Well, I'll start going to that church!" Here's where you let them know you've done your homework on Theresa. Try responding, "When you join that church and abide by their principles, as Theresa is doing, come and see me and I'll see what we can do." What's the likelihood that every one on your staff is going to join the same church and pass muster with the church's leaders as committed and genuinely involved? Even if they did, remember that you as the employer only have to make a reasonable accommodation to the point of undue hardship. If no one could cover the required shifts, you would be looking for different alternatives. But it will never happen. Usually, people blow off a little steam, then come to realize that there are flexible policies in their workplace.

Tip #10 Discrimination can be direct or indirect

When people think about discrimination, they usually think about direct discrimination-as in, "I won't hire any women." However, discrimination can also be indirect; it's then called "adverse effect," "adverse impact" or "indirect discrimination". It's characterized by an employer with a policy that applies to everyone equally, but has an undue negative impact on those with certain human rights characteristics. Let's say your policy is, "I'll hire only people at least six feet tall." Not only does this discriminate against people under six feet; it negatively impacts women more than men. As well, it negatively impacts men and women from countries or regions of the world where individuals are typically not as tall as in Canada. Height is not a protected human rights ground, but sex, ancestry and place of origin are.

> Indirect discrimination applies equally, but has an undue negative impact on certain people

Tip #11 Standards must be legitimate

But what if you *need* tall people for your workplace? If you can justify it as a legitimate job requirement, you are in a better position. This "legitimate" job requirement is often referred to as a bona fide occupational requirement (BFOR). But keep in mind it has to be legit. If your rule lacks merit and someone challenges it, the jig is up.

Tip #12 Accommodate until "undue hardship"

If your policy is found to discriminate against someone on human rights grounds, whether directly or indirectly, you'll have to accommodate that person. How far do you have to go? The courts say up to the point of, or short of, "undue hardship."

Defining "undue hardship" is perplexing at best and uncertain at worst. The Supreme Court of Canada has laid out criteria, while making it clear that their list is not exhaustive; the definition will depend on the facts of each case. In determining undue hardship, the Court has said employers should consider the following:

- Financial cost
- Disruption of a collective agreement

- Problems of morale of other employees
- Interchangeability of workforce and facilities
- Size of the employer's operation
- Safety and who bears the risk

But if you think that a few upset employees, or a frustrated supervisor who has to spend more time figuring out schedules, will constitute undue hardship, you need to think again. The late Supreme Court of Canada Justice John Sopinka dispelled the notion that undue hardship equaled inconvenience when he was writing for the Court in a case regarding a British Columbia school custodian. He said it had to amount to "more than minor inconvenience..." to "actual interference with the rights of other employees, which is not trivial but substantial..." "Minor interference or inconvenience is a price we pay for religious freedom in a multicultural society." [1]

> "Minor interference or inconvenience is a price we pay for religious freedom in a multicultural society."
>
> *Supreme Court Justice John Sopinka*

Tip #13 Re-think policies and procedures

Therefore, from a practical perspective, if you find you have hiring standards, policies, procedures or work rules that may discriminate against someone, look long and hard for a solution. Don't be ready with a "no" just because you haven't done it before, or because it might cause a few workplace wrinkles.

You may be thinking, "How far do I have to go to accommodate? Shouldn't employees have to give a little as well?" You're not alone in your thinking and you're right. The Supreme Court notes that employees also have to be reasonable. Affected employees might not have to come up with a solution to the problem, but if they don't accept a reasonable solution, then the employer has every right

> Employees must also be reasonable in their requests and when looking for resolutions

to deny the requested accommodation. The Court makes it clear that the solution does not have to be "perfect" to be reasonable. If people start digging in their heels over an accommodation, it's best to step back, think rationally and look for a reasoned approach.

Let's return to the case of Theresa, the Seventh-Day Adventist store clerk. Did you do enough to accommodate her religious needs short of undue hardship? Other than giving her a part-time position, you did nothing. You just fell back on the hard and fast rule that everyone has to work most Saturdays and many Friday nights each month. From the court's perspective, you had many options, such as transferring her to other more 9 to 5, Monday-to-Friday jobs. If Theresa wasn't qualified for any of these, what would it have taken to get her qualified? And if retraining her would have created undue hardship, perhaps you needed to have Theresa on the sales floor all but Friday nights and Saturdays. Remember, Theresa could still work Thursday nights.

But you know the real problem. In a world where the majority of people get weekends off, employees aren't happy about one person being accommodated. That's the real reason you didn't create a new shift schedule for Theresa. Don't feel badly, because you were following company policies defended all the way to the Supreme Court of Canada. But now you know better.

Even though today's supervisors, managers, business owners and union shop stewards have some understanding of "reasonable accommodation," the whole notion of it bugs a lot of people. Why should one person, because of religion, disability, sex, family status, or any of the human rights protected grounds, be able to have a different set of work rules when the rest of us have to abide by those same rules? In fact, if we try to assert our so-called "rights" in the same way these few are being accommodated, we will be subject to discipline or termination of employment. It just doesn't seem fair. Those judges on the Supreme Court have no idea what it's like to run a business!

Tip #14 Get employees to understand accommodation

Therein lies your challenge. Like it or not, it's up to you to get your staff to understand the definition of accommodation, and to accept that it is a part of doing business. Here are three suggestions:

- First, don't expect everyone is going to accept it. For many, this is a stellar example of "politically correct bull___". No matter how you explain it, some people won't take kindly to a separate set of rules. That's fine, but don't let someone thwart your workplace requirements under the law. Agreeing to disagree is one thing. Sabotaging a policy set by the Supreme Court of Canada will increase your chances of litigation or bad publicity.

- Second, try to get people to understand that accommodating someone is not the same as allowing her to slack off. It's not a way of milking the system; it's a way of working within the system, within a person's legal rights. Accommodations are not designed to allow an employee to head to the local bar, ski hill or golf course. For most employees, it allows them to honour a higher set of principles or deal with a physical or mental obstacle. In many circumstances, an employer will go to great lengths to check the reality of the request. How involved is this employee with her religion, or does his disability truly put limitations on his ability to do his job? Keep in mind we accommodate employees all the time for items not nearly as serious as faith or injury. If an employee says "I need a Saturday off next month to attend my cousin's wedding in Red Deer," we usually take him at his word and make accommodations when we can.

- Third, let other employees know that if they need an accommodation, it will also be available for them. Portray it as an insurance policy. We all pay insurance every year, hoping we never have to collect. Likewise, should we join a religion, get injured or acquire some other set of circumstances requiring special policies, we will be happy that the option is there; it offers peace of mind.

One of the toughest "sells" I encountered for accommodating an employee involved a worker who was getting out of six months in jail after a conviction for sexually molesting his own children. At that time, the lawyers for the business and the union were unable to find a legitimate reason to keep him from his job, since his criminal conviction was not related to his employment as per the B.C. Human Rights Code. (Much later, in 2003 the Supreme Court of Canada said employers didn't have to keep jobs open for people in jail.) Professionals deemed him no harm to women or men at work, and he readily admitted the harm he did to his (ex) family and his desire to continue seeking treatment. The employer hired me to come and explain the reason for this employee's return, and suggest how people should conduct themselves around him.

The employer and the union didn't expect full buy-in and they weren't surprised by the response. Most people took the information in stride, while others were furious. I told employees they didn't need to befriend this man, but they had to work with him. If they absolutely could not, the employer was willing to consider accommodating different shifts. Luckily, few workplaces will find themselves dealing with an issue as difficult as this one, but those that do should expect emotions to run high.

Getting back to more typical examples, where your human rights jurisdiction has "family status" in its human rights legislation you might need to accommodate an employee by offering a shift suited to child or parental care needs. If you have two employees who get married while in the same department, you may not be able to invoke a policy that says no married couples can work in the same department. But, perhaps all you need to do is change the reporting structure to avoid conflicts of interest.

Tip #15 Accommodate for a changing population

That being said, most of the need for accommodation entails disability and religion. With these two grounds, you'd better be open minded, because you'll be seeing a lot more of them.

Take, for example, disabilities. In years past, persons with disabilities had limited opportunities to get around and were expected to stay in their homes or institutions. In my youth, I remember hearing radio broadcasters in Winnipeg refer to people as "shut-ins". I pictured an old person with limited mobility in a dark room, staring out the window through a small crack in the drapes. In reality, I saw few people with disabilities in the general population, and when I did, I didn't know what to make of them.

> Most accommodations are based on disability and religious grounds

We've come a long way since then, first in the technology and equipment that allows more people to get around, and second, in our accepting people with differences into the general population. The walker, in various forms, has made a huge difference in allowing thousands to have the stability and confidence to go outside and carry on basic tasks such as grocery shopping and mailing a letter.

Advances in technology and treatment are allowing people to work and consume in ways never imagined in the past. As we age, more of us have disabilities. According to census data, while young adults ages 15 to 24 have a disability rate of only 4%, that number increases to 16.7% for the age group 45 to 64. Given our aging population, more of our employment and customer pool will have disabilities in the future. In 2001, Canada's median age was 37.6 years (half the population older and half younger), up 2.3 years from 1996-the biggest census-to-census increase in a century.

As well, for financial or personal reasons, more people are opting to work beyond the age of 65. In the age group 65 to 74, 31.2% of the population has a disability in one form or another. Hence, finding ways to accommodate persons with disabilities is an issue of growing importance. The Federal Human Rights Commission figures more people are starting to assert their rights regarding accommodation by the increase in their numbers of complaints in the categories of age and disability. Between 2001 and 2002, the number of complaints citing

> At the federal level, age discrimination complaints rose 71% and disability complaints rose a whopping 85%

age discrimination rose 71% while disability complaints rose a whopping 85%.

The other major accommodation ground is religion. Since we are a country with many traditions based on the majority-observed Christian religion, sometimes it's hard to see that non-Christians merely want the same kinds of accommodations that Christians have taken for granted for years.

While most Canadians still identify themselves as Christian-43% Roman Catholic and 29% Protestant, for a total of 72% of the population according to the 2001 Census-Christianity has declined as an overall percentage, with the largest increase involving Muslims, Hindus, Sikhs and Buddhists. In one decade, the number of Muslims doubled to 579,600, or 2% of the population. Hindus and Sikhs increased by 89% each for a total of 297,200 and 278,400 respectively, while Buddhists increased by 84% for a total of 300,300. Hindus, Sikhs and Buddhists each make up approximately 1% of the Canadian population.

> The fastest growing religious groups in Canada are Muslims, Hindus, Sikhs and Buddhists

Immigration patterns within Canada are driving this changing demographic. With ever more immigrants arriving from Asia and the Middle East, these religions will continue to grow. Since their members are younger than those in the traditional Catholic and Protestant population, they will have a strong influence on the workplace, especially in geographical pockets where they take up residence. Ontario has 38% of all Canadian Sikhs, 61% of Muslims and 73% of Hindus. About half of the Sikh population lives in British Columbia.

While some employers think of these numbers as small, note that the numbers are growing, and more people are asserting the basic rights that our courts have awarded and our governments have legislated.

Here's another interesting statistic from the 2001 census. While less than 1% of Canadians reported having no religion in 1971, by 2001 that number increased to 16%, or 4.8 million people. Much of this can be traced to immigrants coming from China, Hong Kong and Taiwan in recent years. British Columbia has more people identifying themselves with no religion than any other religious denomination (no religion, 35%; Protestants, 31%; and Catholics, 17%). Alberta, perceived to be Canada's bible belt, came in second, with 23% saying they have no religion. Only 2% of people living in Newfoundland and Labrador said they have no religion.

Since those with no religion are younger than the general population, we can expect the number of Canadians without religious affiliation to grow. It will be interesting to see how this

> What happens if people with no religion want days off in lieu of religious holidays?

impacts our perception of accommodations for religious purposes, as well as the need to ardently adhere to religious statutory holidays in the workplace. Employees still like long weekends on statutory holidays, but more might start asking for alternative days off to add some flexibility to their schedules and address business operational concerns.

Most people don't think of Christians as being accommodated, and yet that is what our Canadian institutions and governments have done for years. For example, look at Sundays. Until recently, virtually everything shut down on Sundays, in keeping with the Christian tradition of resting on the Sabbath. I remember as a kid going across the street after Sunday school with my friends to get chips and a Coke from Lee's Diner. Our mothers must have given us enough money for both the collection plate and the treats. The only Chinese family in that small prairie town, the Lees, worked seven days a week. Their hours were an anomaly, because on Sundays, most businesses and all retailers closed up, giving the town a ghost-like quality. As per the laws of the day, most businesses had to shut down.

Consider how statutory holidays fit into this equation. While New Year's Day, Victoria Day, Canada Day, Labour Day and even Thanksgiving aren't religious holidays, most everything shuts down for Christmas and Easter, the most important of the Christian celebrations. As a Muslim, atheist, Jew or Buddhist, go ahead and try to carry on business as usual in Canada on those days. Everyone accommodates Christians on these important Canadian statutory holidays, regardless of a person's religion or lack thereof.

Tip #16 "Majority rules" doesn't apply to human rights

In defense of these Christian accommodations, people often talk about how the "majority rules." They claim that the reason businesses observe Christian holidays is that the majority of the population adheres to them. That can work in a homogeneous society, but ever since Canada opened its doors to people of all backgrounds and faiths, and ever since the equality provisions of the Charter of Rights and Freedoms came into effect, that sort of logic carries less weight. Before this time, those who did not form part of the majority had no choice but to go along with the laws that had a negative impact on them. "Majority rules" can be great if you are part of the majority. It can suck if you are in the minority. Worse, if others think your observances are a bit strange, good luck being accommodated, even in the 21st Century.

> "Majority rules" can be great if you are in the majority, but it can suck if you are in the minority.

For example, one morning prior to a training session, I read the following *National Post* headline: "Drugstore to pay Jehovah's Witness $30,000 over Christmas display dispute." This isn't good, I thought. Sure enough, the moment I got into the training facility, a few guys were all over me about this article. This was a perfect example, they said, of how human rights is completely out of hand. They didn't like the fact that this employee received $30,000 for refusing to put out six poinsettias during Christmas.

The next day, the *Vancouver Sun* devoted an editorial to the issue, entitled "Human Rights Folly". The paper called it a "silly situation" that "undermines the credibility of legitimate human rights concerns." Even today, newspaper columnists continue to refer to this case as an example of why we need to scrap or significantly change our human rights process, and where things have gone too far.

Let's look at the details of this case and see what the courts had in mind.

Poinsettias and a Jehovah's Witness

Ray Jones had worked at the downtown Shoppers Drug Mart in Victoria, British Columbia for sixteen years between 1982 and 1998. Baptized as a Jehovah's Witness, Jones was an elder in the church. He attended three Witness meetings a week and considered his faith the "most important thing in my life."

Harold Eisler, through his company C.H.E. Pharmacy Inc., became owner of the store in 1988, and always accommodated Jones' religious convictions. Jones' shifts would be scheduled to allow him to attend church meetings, spend time with his family, and attend a Jehovah's Witness convention each year.

Jones had started work as a merchandiser, where his major task was putting merchandise on the shelves. In September 1998, just two months before he left Shoppers for good, Jones was offered the position of cashier supervisor because the company needed better front-end customer service attention, and Jones was very good at customer relations. However, Jones liked his merchandising work and didn't want to take the job. After some discussion, Jones agreed to become a customer service representative, where he would greet and assist customers. When there were few customers around, Jones was allowed to do merchandising.

Ray Jones never had to decorate the store with Christmas decorations, as he did not celebrate Christmas and did not want to promote it. In the early 1990s, Jones went so far as to tell his boss that he did not want to put out Christmas merchandise. He felt this also promoted Christmas. After some discussion, they drew a distinction between handling Christmas and other seasonal merchandise (such as chocolate Easter bunnies), and putting up Christmas decorations. From Jones' perspective, decorating the store for the Christmas holidays would be promoting Christmas, and this was clearly against his faith.

For the 16 years of his employment with Shoppers, Jones was able to avoid the Christmas decorating function because it was voluntary. Only when the decorating function stopped being voluntary in 1998, and everyone was expected to "pitch in," did trouble begin. On November 9 or 10 of that year, Jones' direct supervisor, Don Hardy asked him to hang some garlands in the store. Jones tried to get another merchandiser to do so, but the merchandiser was too busy. So Jones hung the garland, but couldn't believe he had done this after being a Witness for so many years. He had felt that if he didn't do this task, he would lose his job. Now he felt sick. He obviously decided that after sixteen years of his religion being respected, he wouldn't do that again. On November 12th, Hardy asked Jones to hang a cardboard Santa Claus. When Jones refused, Hardy did it himself.

November 17, 1998, Hardy asked Jones to put out six artificial poinsettias. When Jones responded, "Don't go there," Hardy put them out himself-a task that took ten seconds. Later that afternoon, Jones was called into a meeting with his supervisor and the store owner, Harold Eisler. Eisler told Jones he had to follow his supervisor's orders. Jones refused because of his religious convictions and after some discussion, he cleaned out his locker and left. When Hardy saw him at his locker, he said, "What the hell are you doing? This isn't a good decision. You have a family to support."

A couple of days later, in telephone conversations initiated by Jones, he was told that religious beliefs should not be part of the workplace, and that he was not going to get "preferential treatment" because of his religion. Eisler told Jones that he "should be able to ask any employee to do anything whatsoever, without consideration for their religious point of view," and that the company had a "religion-neutral policy".

When you read about this case, which sounds more bizarre: that Jones would quit his job over a few poinsettias, or that the owner and supervisor would dig in their heels over a task that took ten seconds to accomplish?

Tip #17 Accommodations impact your business options

When the Supreme Court of Canada states that an employer must make accommodations towards an employee short of "undue hardship," I find it hard to imagine that this poinsettia incident would be considered an undue hardship to the supervisor, the owner, or any other employee in the store. The courts want businesses to find a way to employ and offer services to people who don't fit the same mold as everyone else. If, in the process, we have to make some changes, so be it. Let's be clear: Human rights legislation puts limits on the way you can run your business. The court makes it clear that businesses must make accommodations to both employees and clients.

Here are just a few examples from the courts and human rights tribunals where a business was required to find a reasonable accommodation to the point of undue hardship. In many cases, undue hardship has been difficult to prove.

• Three Jewish teachers-Joseph Kadoch, Louise Elbraz and Jacob Lahmi-working for the Quebec school board in Chambly, were allowed to take a day's leave of absence, without pay, to celebrate Yom Kippur. They wanted to be paid for the day and grieved under provisions of the collective agreement. At the Supreme Court of Canada, the Court held that the school board must pay

27

for the day off because they had not shown that doing so would constitute an unreasonable financial burden.[2]

- Larry Renaud, a custodian of Seventh-Day Adventist faith, could not work the usual Monday to Friday night after-school shift because his Sabbath started at sunset Friday. The Central Okanagan School District, in B.C's interior, proposed an alternate Sunday to Thursday shift, but his CUPE Local 523 threatened to grieve if the shift change was implemented. Without this agreement from the union, the school board let Renaud go. At the Supreme Court of Canada, the school board and union were both found liable for not accommodating the religious practices of the employee. The ruling stated that the cost of defending a grievance would not have created an undue hardship for the school board, and made it clear that a collective agreement or contract cannot get in the way of human rights legislation.[3]

- Barbara Turnbull and four other persons in wheelchairs were impacted by a policy of Famous Players, a theatre chain, to exclude persons in wheelchairs at three "inaccessible" theatres in Toronto. The Ontario Human Rights Board of Inquiry found in favour of the complainants and ordered the company to make the three theatres accessible within two years of the decision, pay the complainants tens of thousands of dollars in damages, and review their training program for providing services for persons with disabilities. The Board also ordered, "Any film being shown exclusively at those three inaccessible theatres shall be made available to a patron using a wheelchair, upon that person's request of Famous Players, at an accessible theatre to be agreed to by that person and Famous Players." In the end, Famous Players decided to close the theatres. However, before the final theatre was closed, they had to go through a second hearing to take care of the four-month gap between the time the renovations were to have been completed and the date the theatre closed.[4]

- René Poulin was injured on the job while driving a haul truck for the coal mining company, Quintette Operating Corporation. With a generous program for getting injured employees back into the workforce, Quintette gave Poulin modified work while still issuing his regular pay. After more than a year, during which he and his doctor met with the Workers Compensation Board, Poulin accepted the job of building maintenance worker, which paid about $3 an hour less than his truck driving job. The adjudicator said that Quintette treated Poulin "fairly well" throughout, and "acted reasonably" in many different respects. However, because the firm didn't wait for appropriate jobs to become vacant, they didn't accommodate him to the point of undue hardship.[5]

- Katherine Crabtree felt she was discriminated against during an interview for the job of front counter sales person/typesetter at a printing business, Econoprint (Stoney Creek). Once the owner, Stephen Price, asked her about her disability, spinal muscular atrophy, he focused on the difficulty of the job and declined to see her portfolio of work from the college program she was just completing. The Ontario Human Rights adjudicator found that Price was using his own immediate impressions instead of any objective standards to determine if she was capable of doing the job. Price was described as a good employer who had no bias against disabled employees, but he could have accommodated Crabtree with minimal business expense.[6]

- Terry Grismer was a mining truck driver from the interior of British Columbia, who after a stroke suffered from homonymous hemianopia (H.H.). H.H. took away Grismer's left-side vision in both eyes, which in turn led the B.C. Motor Vehicles Branch to cancel his driver's licence. The average person has a 200 to 220 degree field of vision, and the B.C. Superintendent of Motor Vehicles imposes a standard of a minimum 120 degree field of vision. People with H.H. have less than a 120 degree field of vision, and therefore are prohibited from driving in

B.C. There are no exceptions, even though Grismer was able to pass his tests four times over a seven-year period because he devised ways to compensate for his lack of peripheral vision. A unanimous Supreme Court of Canada upheld the right of people with H.H. to ask for a driving assessment and not be dismissed out of hand.[7] (Sadly, Grismer died years before this decision was rendered.)

There are also examples where the employer is able to prove undue hardship - where the employer did not have to make an accommodation even though it meant discriminating against the employee.

- Darshan Singh Pannu worked for the pulp mill Skeena Cellulose in British Columbia. As a recaust operator, he worked in the part of the mill where poisonous gases are piped in to burn off in 2,000-degree recaust kilns. In the event of a gas leak, he was responsible for wearing a mask - a self-contained breathing apparatus - to protect him while doing an emergency shutdown of the recaust area equipment while others evacuate. However, as a Sikh who wears a beard as part of his faith, Pannu was unable to create a tight seal to his face as required by the Workers' Compensation Board. The human rights adjudicator found that in the event of an emergency, Pannu would be putting not only himself at risk, but others in the mill, and as such, that created an undue hardship for Skeena to accommodate Pannu in that particular job. Hence, they were allowed to discriminate against him based on his religion, for the purposes of this job.[8]

- Sidney MacEachern worked as a stationary engineer in the boiler plant at St. Francis Xavier University in Antigonish, Nova Scotia before joining the World Wide Church of God. His need for strict observance of their Sabbath from sundown Friday to sundown Saturday, along with eight holy days in the spring and fall, greatly conflicted with his twelve-hour rotating shifts. The adjudicator went through most of the Supreme Court of

Canada's factors to determine if accommodation was possible, such as cost, safety, morale, etc. In the end, the adjudicator concluded that accommodating MacEachern would have been an undue hardship on the university. A key factor in this case was the small size of the university, where having to take on another engineer's salary would have caused undue hardship. A larger university may have ended up with a different result.[9]

• Karen Harris was a student at Victoria's Camosun College's criminology program. She and the college agreed that she had developed multiple chemical and environmental sensitivities that prevented her from attending certain classrooms. Harris was able to work out agreements to sit near the window for some classes, and to tape others, or have people take notes for her. However, three courses needed class participation and some kind of activity on the part of the student. With one course in particular, Psychology 154/Interpersonal Relations, the stated objectives of class included experiential learning that could be achieved only through group classroom participation. The adjudicator found that the college could not have reasonably accommodated Harris's desire to tape the class without creating undue hardship. [10]

Tip #18 Broaden your view of accommodations

If, after reading about these cases, you are confused, don't panic. For years, employers, employees, unions, lawyers and scholars have been debating how far employers and businesses have to go to accommodate people. The list of criteria noted at the beginning of this chapter by the Supreme Court of Canada isn't exact and does not give people a lot with which to work. But just because we are confused, doesn't mean we can throw up our arms in frustration when we are confronted with a possible accommodation issue.

My challenge to today's managers is to take a wide

view of what constitutes an accommodation, to put your-self in the shoes of another person, even if just for a moment. And if you think Canada has gone as far as it can go on this issue, think again.

The trends marked by the cases I've mentioned have evolved over the years, and the courts are becoming more progressive in finding ways to accommodate people with differences who don't fit our sometimes neat and tidy rules and policies. One case in particular has moved the process to a new level. On September 9, 1999, in a unanimous decision, the Supreme Court of Canada got rid of some of the more perplexing interpretations of accommodation and made it easier to understand-that is, from a legal interpre-tation. With this case, the government moved the pendulum even further to accommodate differences in the workplace. Many human rights adjudicators and lawyers have picked up on this, but I don't think employers in the rest of the country have recognized the importance of this decision or how it will impact the way businesses must treat people who don't fall into the majority.

> The Supreme Court recently moved the pendulum even further to accommodate differences

Tawney Meiorin was hired as a forest firefighter in the early 1990s, working for the British Columbia Ministry of Forests. Her work performance was satisfactory, but after she had spent a few years on the job, and in response to a coroner's inquest, all employees were required to pass a series of tests. Meiorin passed three, but did not pass the fourth, a 2.5-km run designed to test her aerobic abilities. After four tries, she still took 49.4 seconds longer than the required time of 11 minutes, and was let go. Her union got her job back at arbitration, and that decision was eventu-ally supported by the Supreme Court of Canada. Meiorin, meanwhile, ended up taking a job as a lumberjack and never returned to the Forest Service.

With this decision, the Court adopted a three-step test to find out if a discriminatory "standard" (action, poli-cy, requirement, etc.) is in fact a legitimate occupational requirement. With this test, an employer has to establish that their standard is related to the job, is done in good faith and can't be accommodated in some way. Take note of what was said about undue hardship: "To show that the standard is reasonably necessary, it must be demonstrated that it is *impossible* to accommodate individual employees sharing the characteristics of the claimant without imposing undue hardship upon the employer." [11] [emphasis added]

Notice how they said it must be "impossible" to accommodate an employee to the point of undue hardship? In my opinion, the court is saying, "You'd better look long and hard to accommodate differences."

In the body of the decision, Justice McLachlin (now Chief Justice) went beyond the facts of the case for Meiorin and delved into the bigger picture of why we need to accommodate differences and why we need to stop trying to assimilate people into positions that just won't fit. I feel the court is sending a message that says we need to look at all Canadians as equal, and stop thinking, "Aren't I nice for accommodating you if you aren't 'normal'?" I think the court is saying, "Don't complain when someone asks your business to fund wheelchair access; think, 'Why did I create access only to people who can walk in the first place?'" The courts and adjudicators, following their lead, will find it increasingly difficult to sympathize with an employer who claims it's an undue hardship to accommodate someone.

This big step was reflected three months later in the case of Grismer, the man who wanted to get his driver's license even though he had homonymous hemianopia. Justice McLachlin, speaking for a unanimous court, not only upheld the right for someone like Grismer to ask for a driving assessment, but she added that "the thrust of human rights legislation is to eliminate the assumption...[that] persons with disabilities are unable to accomplish certain tasks"

> "It's all too easy to cite increased cost as a reason for refusing to accord the disabled equal treatment"
>
> *Chief Justice Beverly McLachlin*

33

and to break down the barriers that stand in the way of equality for all. "It's all too easy to cite increased cost as a reason for refusing to accord the disabled equal treatment," she stated.

Tip #19 Making accommodations is not being charitable

I interpret these statements as a warning to employers and service providers that accommodation, especially for persons with disabilities, is no longer being seen as being charitable. It is and will continue to be a requirement. Businesses will have a tougher time refusing jobs and services to people unless they can show there is no chance of accommodating those differences.

Mr. Jones & Shoppers Drug Mart revisited

A few pages back, I asked which you thought was more bizarre, that Raymond Jones would quit his job over a few poinsettias, or that the owner and supervisor would dig in their heels over a ten second task.

From what you know now of the direction the Supreme Court of Canada is heading (whether or not you agree with their direction), you know that the Shoppers Drug Mart store owner and supervisor should have found a way to accommodate Jones. In fact, of all the cases noted above, this case would have involved the easiest of accommodations. Unfortunately, Eisler and Hardy were focused on the insubordination instead of the wider issue of religious accommodation. It's a lesson we can all take to heart.

Just so you know, the Jones case was one of "constructive dismissal." By that I mean Jones was compensated for leaving his job for refusing to do a task that he and his employer had agreed he did not have to do during the previous sixteen years. By law, you can let an employee go if he is unwilling to change a fundamental aspect of his job, but you've got to pay him reasonable notice. In this case, the headline-grabbing $30,000 award was in fact $27,095.96 for loss of income, vacation pay, interest and expenses, while only $3,500 was paid for "injury to his dignity, feelings and self respect."

I agree with the tribunal's adjudicator, Tom Patch, who wrote, "This is an unfortunate case." Jones was clearly a valued employee who, when he had problems with his bosses, had until then been able to work them out.

I spoke with both Jones and Eisler separately, expecting each to say bad things about one another. I was surprised at the level of mutual respect and the civility with which each spoke of their working relationship. Eisler said, "Ray was damn good with customers." Jones said "I had a good rapport with Harold." Yet both of them brought up personal stories indicating feelings of hurt or betrayal over what transpired.

Jones told me "When this first happened, I called Shoppers Human Resources in Vancouver and spoke to a fellow. They never called me back or said anything after 16 years. Pretty sad, huh?"

Harold Eisler asked my opinion, after noting that the whole thing cost him approximately $45,000 plus his down time with the lawyers and at the hearing. I told him I thought it was a hefty price to pay just to make sure Ray Jones put out a few poinsettias, and it was an unfortunate way to lose a valuable employee.

Tip #20 Accommodate regardless of personal values

What makes religious accommodation difficult is we know so little about religions beyond our own. Regardless of our own upbringing, we have a reasonable understanding of Canada's major religions-Christianity and Judaism. We are not willing to accommodate those we know very little about. In many circles, Jehovah's Witnesses remain the butt of jokes and ridicule.

But that's the kicker. We are being asked to accept and understand people in the minority with increasing frequency, and some of what they believe will go against our basic beliefs and values. We are being asked to challenge what we know. If we're wise, we'll meet that challenge.

Parting Tips for Are You Accommodating?

Tip #21 Don't make assumptions about dis/abilities

Don't assume you know what people can and can't do as a result of their disabilities. Ask them. As you do with other job candidates, determine their qualifications and abilities. We tend to expect some poetic license from résumés and interviews, yet we take people at their word on how they're going to fit into the job for which they are being considered. References help, and you always have the probationary period, so if the person doesn't pan out, you can part ways. Apply the same process for someone with a disability.

Tip #22 Find ways to soften the financial burden

Many accommodations cost no money at all. Some take organizational time and others involve flexibility on the part of employees and employers. Then again, some accommodations will incur costs. Financial assistance or equipment from a government or non-governmental agency sometimes helps. Don't assume you have to do it all yourself. Human Resources Development Canada has provided money to provincial and non-governmental agencies to help defray the costs of some accommodations that cost money.

Even the Canadian government's Canada Mortgage & Housing Corporation offers forgivable loans to landlords to make rental housing accessible to people with disabilities.

Tip #23 Train supervisors about accommodations

Make sure decision-makers-supervisors and anyone who makes decisions about employment and customer service-know about the legal requirement to accommodate employees, potential employees and customers. Many accommodations require adapting rules, but such decisions can be made on the spot. Others need more thought applied to the process, cost and safety. Help your organization spell these things out, and then relay them to your decision makers in bulletins, one-on-one discussions and group training sessions. Don't wait until you've gone through a nasty and costly legal process to inform people in your organization.

Tip #24 Keep employees informed

If you want to be highly proactive, let all employees know about the legal need to accommodate. It doesn't have to come through a separate training session. It can be communicated through a staff bulletin or as part of a regular update of employment information. I know this brings up anxiety about floodgate theories, where once everyone knows about it, they'll all want to be accommodated. But, trust me: People don't run out to join a religion or find new injuries once they learn such things are accommodated.

If you don't want to be proactive, at least properly communicate the situation and the supportive resolution when the time comes. And I mean *supportive*. Too often I've heard supervisors who have grudgingly explained a "ridiculous" resolution imposed by the employer and, if relevant, the union. When there are groans from this level, you can practically hear the sympathy groans likely to emanate one layer down from the so-called team leaders. If the person issuing the communication can't be supportive, find someone who is. Where there is no real support for an accommodation, sabotaging knives will appear. And that's not likely a scenario you want to confront.

Tip #25 Adapt now to avoid future problems

So now you know that as you make operational business decisions, you can't assume that everyone walks as fast as you, can get to work at the same time or will be celebrating the same holidays. Already, as buildings are built or re-modeled, government agencies ensure there is more accessibility than in the past, thereby averting some of today's problems. And for the future you will be well-advised to keep new clients and employees in mind at all times. On average, they will be older than in years past, and therefore more likely to be coping with some kind of a disability. More and more are immigrants likely to celebrate different days than yesterday's workforce. Why waste time fighting it? We are all best served by spending time finding ways to work with the new realities.

"If a million people say a foolish thing, it is still a foolish thing."

Anatole France

3

Harassment Headaches

Harassment: A thing of the past. No longer a problem. Why worry about it? Took the course, heard the message, bought the T-shirt. In the States, multi-million dollar sexual harassment lawsuits hardly get notice anymore. In five short paragraphs, in the less-than-prominent "Careers" section of the *Vancouver Sun,* here was the headline for May 3, 2003: "Dial Corp. Settles Sex Harassment Suit". The article was so obscure and tiny, you'd think the soap-making corporation had merely received a slap on the wrist. In fact, the article noted that Dial paid $10 million dollars over allegations of sexual harassment.

Here in Canada, as most of us know, huge harassment payouts don't happen. But on a per capita basis, Canada must have as many harassment issues as the States, which means the issue of harassment harms employee morale and retention, and an organization's bottom line. In Canada, as in the United States, harassment is bad for business.

It is 1974 and Carole, her husband and children move to a town in B.C. after her husband loses his job in Ontario. After three months of looking, she gets a job with a private company as executive secretary to the president, Wayne. Even before she gets the job, the sexual comments start. He says that by analyzing her handwriting, he can tell that she is unhappy in her marriage and the type of person to enjoy sex acts. She ignores this and gets the job. After she starts work, Wayne tells Carole he hired her to "help him with his sexual needs" and expresses confidence that she will be a "good bedfellow".

Part of Carole's job is traveling with Wayne on business trips by car. As they drive, he often talks of his "sex addiction" and how he wants a "special relationship" with her, since they will be away on business frequently. Wayne explains that he has had these special relationships with others in the past. When they get to their destination, their hotel rooms are adjoining and Wayne tells her the door between the rooms has to remain unlocked "in case he needs her to take dictation". On that first night, she is called into his room to take dictation. Wayne is in his underwear. As he presses his body against hers, Wayne says she excites him and he just wants to get into bed with her. Although she knows she risks her only family income by doing so, she refuses.

On the same trip, at a restaurant, Wayne tells Carole to sit next to him, instead of opposite. During the trip, he rubs her arms, smells her hair and gives her "little kisses" on the top of her head. He tells her that if she keeps quiet about these attempts, her job is secure.

There are other business trips with similar harassment. Wayne tells Carole that he can't concentrate on his job because he is "wild with lust" for her. At one point, he asks Carole if she will spank his buttocks while he masturbates. Horrified, she declines. He tells her he is "not the type of person who would go into your room and ejaculate while you are not there". He continues to make these and other very direct advances at her. When she does not comply, he tells her that her job is in jeopardy and he is angry with her. Back at the office, Wayne's conversations include sexual banter.

Wayne's conduct has a negative impact on Carole's relationship with her family. She becomes tired, depressed and withdrawn. She has difficulty concentrating and becomes nervous about going to work. After six and a half months on the job, Carole discusses her situation with her family doctor and quits her job. She is referred to the Community Mental Health Office and goes on medication for nerves and insomnia for a year.

Once she's out of work, Carole and her family end up on welfare and cash in their life insurance policies. This, she would later tell the tribunal, "took all the dignity out of me". Eight and a half months later, Carole began work with another company.

When we read Carole's case, many of us are probably thinking, "Why would she put up with that stuff?" and "Thank goodness that doesn't happen anymore."

But when we let ourselves fall into the trap of asking why Carole or anyone else puts up with sexual harassment, we are putting our focus in the wrong place. At all times, we need to ask, "Why was Wayne allowed to get away with this?" Carole made it clear she didn't want that kind of attention from Wayne, but only a guy with a brain like a wooden plank would need to be told so. A person with an ounce of decency would neither do what Wayne did, nor need to be told his actions are wrong. Wayne knew Carole was powerless because of her need to feed and care for her family. He knew full well what he was doing. Carole was desperate enough to stick it out for the sake of her family. In so doing, she suffered a terrible impact on her health and well-being.

On the second point-"thank goodness that doesn't happen anymore"-I have to make a confession. This didn't happen to Carole in 1974. It happened to another woman in 1994 and 1995 in the city of Nelson, B.C. Wayne Sequin, and his company, Tri Spike Cedar Ltd., which was doing business under the name of Data Secured Ltd., was president. Strangely enough, he not only let this go to a hearing instead of settling at the Human Rights Commission, but he represented himself and did not contradict his former employee's testimony on cross-examination. [12]

Is it difficult to imagine weird sexual harassment cases still taking place in Canadian workplaces? I continue to marvel at the fact that cases like this continue to roll out on a daily basis. And I'm forced to admit that, since most people don't report sexual and other forms of harassment, it's much more prevalent than we imagine. Of course, sexual harassment cases aren't always as obvious and damaging as the one noted above.

Here are some of the most frequently asked questions I get regarding workplace harassment, and my thoughts on the downside of not dealing with harassment.

Is sexual harassment just about sex?

In 1989, then-Chief Justice Brian Dixon of the Supreme Court of Canada, in a unanimous decision, said "sexual harassment in the workplace may be broadly defined as *unwelcome conduct of a sexual nature that detrimentally affects the work environment or leads to adverse job-related consequences for the victims of the harassment.* It is...an abuse of power...[that] attacks the dignity and self-respect of the victim both as an employee and as a human being."[13] (emphasis added)

Today, the italicized part of that decision serves to define sexual harassment in Canada. To prove sexual harassment, a person needs to show he or she endured unwelcome sexual attention and that it had detrimental or negative consequences. While the consequences can be the classic, "You show me some sexual attention and I'll let you keep your job," they don't have to go that far. A person who endures provocative pictures on the wall, or sexual jokes told in the lunchroom is often a person being subjected to sexual harassment. This is often referred to as a tainted, poisoned or hostile work environment.

Tip #26 Sexual harassment isn't just about sex

Since the courts have ruled that sexual harassment is a form of sex discrimination, treating women negatively while treating men positively can constitute sexual harassment. In other words, if snide or rude comments are made to women but not to men, and they negatively impact the women's workplace comfort level, this is sexual harassment. The reverse is also true if men are the predominant targets.

My advice is to think of sexual harassment as more than the textbook case of a lecherous male boss. Non-sexual negative comments towards one particular gender, or a man harassing a man, or a woman harassing a woman all qualify. That said, it should come as no surprise that most sexual harassment still involves a man sexually harassing a woman.

What kinds of harassment are there?

Since the courts have ruled that sexual harassment is a form of discrimination based on sex (or gender), they have continued to interpret harassment to include other protected forms of discrimination covered under human rights legislation. What other types? Depending on the provincial, territorial or federal human rights legislation, your list is made up from a number of the protected grounds noted below:

Age	Physical disability	Ancestry
Sex	Criminal conviction	Political belief
Race	Aboriginal origin	Marital status
Gender	Social condition	Family status
Colour	Sexual orientation	Language
Creed	Mental disability	Citizenship
Religion	Source of income	Civil status
Ethnicity	Linguistic background	Nationality
Pregnancy	Irrational fear of illness or disease	Place of origin

Tip #27 Harassment protections are varied

If an employee is being harassed, but that harassment doesn't qualify under the protected grounds of discrimination, the human rights commission will not be able to legally assist that employee. The person being harassed and her employer will want to deal with the problem somehow, but it won't be through human rights.

43

Human rights commissions are designed to take care only of issues under their jurisdictions-not all problems that ails us.

If a provincial, territorial or federal commission does not offer all the protected grounds, be aware that a person can argue a new case to forge new ground. In Alberta, Delwin Vriend was fired from his job because he was gay. Since sexual orientation was not a protected ground in Alberta, Vriend was unable initially to secure protection from the province's human rights commission. But after many appeals, the Supreme Court of Canada "read in" protection of sexual orientation to the province's legislation, and the province did not attempt to overturn the decision. So even though you don't see sexual orientation listed as a category in Alberta, Alberta's Human Rights and Citizenship Commission has made it clear that heterosexual men and women, gay men, lesbians and bisexual men and women will get protection if they have a complaint based on their sexual orientation.

> Courts can "read in" new human rights categories, so the legislated list isn't final.

If I were in charge of a business, I wouldn't lose sleep over whether an employee might end up influencing the Supreme Court to change laws, but I would make sure employees don't feel they have to go elsewhere to resolve internal matters. Just because harassment based on hair loss is not protected by law doesn't mean you should allow one employee to call another employee "cue-ball."

Doesn't someone have to tell me I'm harassing him, before it can be considered harassment?

No. The legal standard for everyone involved is that harassment may exist even if you don't think of it as harassment.

Tip #28 Harassment can take place without a complaint

If an adjudicator thinks you should have known, that's enough to plow full speed ahead, legally. A supervisor, manager or owner who attempts a defense by saying he didn't know that pictures of nude women or men would be a problem to some employees will get nowhere. Might as well try saying, "I've been living under a rock."

It works the same way in non-harassment cases. An employer who tells the Workers' Compensation Board, "I didn't know that water on the floor might cause an employee to slip and fall" is wasting her breath.

For those who feel this has an element of unfairness, keep in mind that a finding of harassment rarely spells the end of someone's career; it doesn't even have to entail discipline. It remains a last-resort measure to fire an employee due to harassment.

Need an example? Let's say I like to talk about my sexual exploits with colleagues in the workplace lunchroom. Since no one objects, I assume everyone wants to hear my stories. It also happens that I have a reasonable amount of clout at work, and one of my colleagues dislikes my stories but dares not say so for fear I might retaliate. That colleague may go to our boss and ask him to deal with the issue. When the boss tells me I have to knock off the sexual stories, my ego will feel a bit bruised, but if I agree to stop with the lunchtime stories, it's most likely an end to the problem. The other guy just wants to keep his lunch down; he's not looking to get me fired or himself compensation.

It's a simple example, but for every complex harassment case, there are twenty to forty easily resolved incidents such as this one. That's where you come in. You're the boss being asked to tell Big Mouth me "enough already" on the tacky lunch-hour bragging. You're the one in a position to stop twenty incidents from inflating into workplace dilemmas or legal cases.

Tip #29 A complaint shouldn't kill a career

Your simple response to this one-having a word with me in our example above-also falls within the law. Human rights legislation is referred to as "remedial" legislation, and it aims to find a reasonable remedy acceptable to most. In fact, if my colleague asked that I be fired for telling a sexual joke, it would be considered out of line from a legal perspective-assuming I wasn't doing anything more serious.

What about "third party" harassment?

So what happens if harassment is overheard by a "third party"-someone to whom the comment or joke wasn't directed? Watch out, because the courts and tribunals aren't interested in creating loopholes.

Tip #30 No loopholes for third party harassment

As per the definition of harassment, if a person hears comments that are unwelcome and cause a negative impact, then you've either got harassment, or the beginnings of harassment. So if you get the sense that your employees assume they can say whatever they want at their desks and in the lunchroom, and tough luck for anyone who happens to be eavesdropping, set them straight. Harassment is harassment and it doesn't matter whether a person is a first, second or third party to the harassment.

Need I worry about harassment if my intentions are good?

Yes. Intentions are irrelevant when deciding if harassment has occurred. My intentions might be to lighten up the workplace by telling sexual jokes, or help myself fit in with the power crowd by belittling people with the same colour skin as mine. I may even think my pictures of nudes-reproductions of classic paintings that people travel to prestigious museums to see-are beautifying our drab workplace walls. But my opinion is my own, and the opinion of my colleagues is what can create harassment at work. *It is the impact, not the intention that matters.*

Tip #31 Focus on impact, not intent

As for employees who tell you, "Oh that's just Stephen; he doesn't mean anything by it," here's what to keep in mind. Good people can say bad things, and you're helping no one by allowing them to get away with comments or conduct that violate the basic rights of others. Again, if you focus your attention on the impact, not the intentions, you're modeling good leadership.

Does intention have any influence at all? Actually, once a finding of harassment has taken place, then intention might go a long way in deciding how to resolve it. If, for example, I harass someone with the intention of inflicting harm or humiliation on that person, and do so with complete disregard for her feelings, I'm likely to be subject to disciplinary action, perhaps even severe discipline.

> Intention can play a part in deciding the remedy, but not the finding, of harassment

However, if colleagues or investigators are convinced that I never intended a negative impact, perhaps I felt silly when I learned what I'd done and was sincerely apologetic, chances are I will not be disciplined. It was still harassment, but being hauled into my supervisor's office for a "discussion" may be considered action enough.

Can my actions be deemed harassment if they occur outside of work?

Yes. If an employee does something outside of work that has a negative impact back in the workplace, the employer may well find himself or herself dealing with a harassment problem. Otherwise, imagine the loopholes, especially given today's technology. Ed would just have to wait until after work to send lewd e-mails, faxes, and voice mail messages to his co-worker Tricia's home. Or leave sexually explicit messages under her car's windshield wipers.

Back at work, of course, Ed acts like a perfect gentleman. But if Tricia is disturbed by his actions, and we apply the definition of sexual harassment, what have we got? An employee receiving sexual attention she doesn't want, with negative consequences: a tainted work environment. Tricia is on edge all the workday wondering what Ed will pull next.

Tip #32 Deal with harassment inside & out

I investigated just such a case for a client. One night after their shift in the company parking lot, an employee asked a female colleague if she'd like a ride home. Having no reason to suspect anything except courtesy from a fellow worker, she accepted the ride. As soon as she noticed he was going in the wrong direction, she asked to be taken home or at least dropped off. He told her he just needed to pick up something from his apartment, then he'd take her home. As soon as he parked the car in his underground garage, she leapt out and escaped. She made her way back to the workplace, completely distraught.

Since she never made it to his apartment, we'll never know what his final motives were. The company hired me to investigate; in the meantime, the male employee was placed on an unpaid leave of absence. His union, protecting his interests, argued that since all of this had happened outside the workplace, it wasn't a workplace harassment case. The union stressed that the woman should have referred it to the police. But I knew the law said otherwise. I suggested termination of employment for the young man, because even if he'd been placed on a different shift from the woman who filed the complaint, I knew she'd never feel comfortable with the notion that she might cross paths with him again on work premises. The company severed his employment, but stipulated that if he underwent counseling and was able to show he was no longer a threat to women in the firm, he could have his job back. He declined to pursue this option, his union's grievance was dropped, and his termination of employment was upheld.

Tip #33 Keep an eye on social functions

Most harassment cases off workplace property are not as severe, and do not end up with a person being fired. In my experience, most involve booze, parties or an infatuation. As comedian Phyllis Diller has said, "What I don't like about office Christmas parties is looking for a job the next day." Perhaps you should encourage the employees under your wing to take that to heart. When companies hire me to train employees about harassment issues, they often ask me to dwell a little on booze and company outings, thanks to unfortunate incidents in their past.

Not that employees shouldn't socialize after hours. When problems do occur, most off-premises conflicts do not involve harassment. Personality conflicts or other problems that don't fit the definition of harassment do not have to be settled with a harassment policy or procedure. You might have a problem on your hands, but it won't be harassment.

Infatuations are particularly tricky to identify and deal with. As often as not, the person needs counseling of some kind. Your role is simply to let the spurned employee know he needs to keep his feelings in check, while ensuring that the object of his desires feels completely comfortable bringing any problem to your attention. You can minimize the chances of off-premises issues becoming a bigger problem by letting employees know even their actions *off* the worksite can become a workplace concern.

Can't an employee use harassment as a way of bringing down the boss or a colleague she doesn't like?

Yes, but it's very, very rare. On a different front, anyone can falsely accuse us of assault; it's a chance we take in a free and democratic system. If it happens, we hope the system works. If a case proves that the system is flawed, we don't shut down the entire criminal justice system; we try to tighten up the loopholes. The bottom line is, the system works most of the time.

Harassment and the human rights process work on the same assumption. If someone knowingly makes a false accusation, most of the time, the system will work. The accusation will be out of line with the character of the supposed harasser, the so-called victim will slip up on some lie, or the accuser will confess.

Tip #34 Ensure consequences for false accusers

The bigger problem is workplaces that fail to deal with harassment complaints. Too often, managers assigned to address the harassment have no idea how to handle it effectively. When they deem something to be a false accusation, they make the mistake of letting it die, thus leaving the wrongfully accused person undisciplined but steaming. For the sake of fairness, employee morale, and avoidance of future such cases, if not for overall honesty's sake, I say it's far better to take stern action against the person who knowingly made the false accusation.

The fact that false accusations are rare is little comfort to those who find themselves falsely accused. In my experience, when a case doesn't progress to the point they can clear their name, or when it takes too long to do so, they feel, rightfully so, that the system isn't working.

If we talk about harassment, won't that just create more complaints?

If it does, it means existing problems are not being addressed. Do we minimize crime prevention campaigns for fear that calling attention to crime might create more crime? No. You want employees to deal with harassment and if the only outlet they feel they can use is through a formal complaint, better you get a chance to deal with it yourself than getting a call from a human rights commission.

The day after a colleague of mine gave a half-day harassment awareness training session to one of his company's offices, *every* female employee in that office filed a complaint of sexual harassment. My friend was in a flap, thinking his firm would be upset at him, and that he'd done something wrong. As it turns out, sexual harassment had been going on long before the trainer ever arrived. All he'd done was instill a belief in these women that the company cared, and let them know there were ways of dealing with their problems. They no longer had to suffer in silence. These women clearly needed an outlet; lucky for the company they found an internal one.

Tip #35 Talk openly for better results

As I mentioned earlier, harassment complaints are still the tip of the iceberg. The vast majority of both severe and minor incidences go unreported. Contrary to what some people would have you believe, most people don't want to make waves or jeopardize their careers, nor do they expect workplace support. Most also believe that their complaints might lead to a colleague being dismissed.

Howard might think Jane is extremely crude, rude and a downright pig, but he knows Jane has kids and makes a decent contribution to the workplace. He'd like to submit a complaint to their common supervisor, but from having watched a news story or two on harassment cases, he assumes this might get her the boot, and he doesn't want that on his conscience. He just wants her to stop making offending remarks. Of course, if he's lucky enough to have you as a supervisor and to have some training on this subject, alerting him to the fact that she probably won't be fired, he'll feel comfortable dropping by and talking to you, resolving it that way.

My advice, clearly, is to make harassment easy (or easier) to talk about. Make sure everyone knows the realistic consequences, and give every complaint the attention it deserves. Most issues can be handled properly without management even knowing about them; it's just a matter of making people feel more comfortable addressing the issues on their own.

Does someone get "charged" with harassment and can a person go to court?

I correct people when they talk about "charges" of harassment. Maybe it's splitting hairs, but I think using the word "charges" instead of "complaints" adds fuel to the fire; it implies that harassment is so severe that people can't tackle it on their own before it reaches a public level.

Under human rights legislation in Canada, a person can suffer a harassment complaint, but not a charge. They will not attain a criminal record or go to jail. They will likely be spoken to, will possibly have to pay damages, might be instructed to take a course or promise to cease and desist with the offending behaviour, and in rare cases, they'll lose their job. There are charges of criminal harassment under the Criminal Code, but that entails severe cases and is the subject for another book.

A harassment complaint will not start at the court level. First it goes to a commission or tribunal, which tries to resolve the problem. If that process is adjudicated or exhausted, someone can appeal to the courts-a lengthy and expensive process, but one available to any of the parties involved.

Tip #36 Complaints can show up elsewhere

Other regulatory quasi-judicial bodies have to deal with issues of harassment when they come up. For example, if someone says harassment is the reason for leaving a job, and they're claiming employment insurance, then the federal Employment Insurance department has to decide if harassment has taken place. If someone is on stress leave due to a harassing work environment, Workers' Compensation will get pulled in. Labour arbitrators often have to decide harassment issues, and the courts deal with wrongful dismissal cases due to harassment all the time.

Who is responsible for harassment?

The Supreme Court of Canada has made it very clear that management is responsible for what goes on in their workplace. From what I've seen, human rights commissions and tribunals take a very liberal definition of management. They don't care if a supervisor is inside or outside a union, or whether she has hiring and firing capabilities. They just want to see someone who supervises employees, deal with harassment.

Tip #37 Liability can be shared

As for unions, in September of 1992, the Supreme Court of Canada made a ruling against both the Canadian Union of Public Employees and the Central Okanagan

School Board in British Columbia, related to a human rights complaint. The case, which involved the need to accommodate a Seventh-Day Adventist employee, ended up being the first time the top court stated that a union had a "shared" duty with an employer to deal with a human rights issue. Since then, unions realized they had more than a moral obligation to work with employers on issues of human rights in the workplace. Even though they are not ultimately responsible for dealing with harassment, they have a legal duty to work with management.

Take, for example, an employee wanting an internal transfer while her complaint of harassment against her boss is completed. There may be an opening in another part of the business, but because of her lack of seniority, she is ineligible for the job placement. In such circumstances, I think the union has to consider this temporary request to support the harassment process, even though it does not follow collective agreement provisions. Many unions were working with management on human rights issues long before the Supreme Court ruling.

Who bears the burden of proof in a harassment case?

As in all human rights issues, there is a bit of a reverse onus. If a complainant makes a prima facie case of harassment, then the onus of proof reverts to the employer who must show that on a balance of probabilities, the harassment did not occur. Prima facie means "at first sight" or "on the face of it".

Tip #38 Reverse onus catches people off-guard

In other words, if I turn up at a human rights commission with a story of being harassed by my boss, and I present to them a poem from my boss, insinuating he's in love with me, my boss will have to show that the harassment wasn't going on, because that's very compelling evidence. If he then shows up and produces a stack of love letters from me to him and explains that it's me who is infatuated with him, and that he sent only one poem in response, meant entirely tongue in cheek, he has a chance of proving this was not harassment. (He'd also prove poor judgment and a lack of careful listening at the last company harassment training session.)

What does it cost to resolve a harassment case?

As a supervisor, if you spot a harassment problem or someone brings it to your attention, and you deal with it immediately, your costs will be negligible. You shouldn't have any out-of-pocket expenses, although it will take some time away from the operational side of your business.

If you ignore a situation and an employee goes to a human rights commission or tribunal, you could be looking at a lot of time and money. You'll certainly end up spending company dollars if, in response to the complaint, you go overboard by firing an employee and it's later determined this was not warranted. It's a bit like Goldie Locks and the Three Bears. It doesn't have to be "just right", but it needs to be close.

If management represents your business without a lawyer, you won't have the legal costs, but the company could rack up tens, and in some cases hundreds, of hours of time defending and explaining harassment allegations. If it is resolved without going to a tribunal (most don't go to a tribunal), you or your business will need to agree to a settlement that might include a financial award and harassment training for some or all of your employees. If the case is settled in your favor, you won't have to pay anything. If you do not settle, and your case goes to

> If your case goes to a tribunal, you will have to wait months for it to be resolved

a tribunal, not only will you have to spend hours and hours preparing for and being present at the hearing, but you will have to endure months and months of waiting for the case to be resolved.

If management gets a lawyer to represent the business, you're looking at an hourly fee of between $150 and $350 per hour-maybe more. When the work begins you don't get to say "please stop at $4,000 since that's all we budgeted". The meter on that fee will run for:

- All meetings in which you explain your side to your lawyer
- The time the lawyer spends preparing and defending your position, *and*
- Her time spent researching the latest legal cases

Rarely are these cases simple. Most are complex on several fronts at once, requiring time to sort through all the players and actions. And don't be surprised to pay a legal bill of between $5,000 and $20,000 to secure a settlement - an amount that does not include any settlement award.

> Settling a case can cost you legal bills of between $5,000 and $20,000 (not including any agreed settlement award)

When you can't settle and you go to a human rights tribunal or a court case (a wrongful dismissal case might be an example of such a situation), depending on the length of the proceedings, your costs can easily exceed $20,000. I recently heard of a wrongful dismissal case at B.C.'s Supreme Court, just a few blocks from my office, where a union had fired one of its business reps for sexual harassment, and he was suing the union for wrongful dismissal. That portion of the case was expected to last ten days alone, and involved two lawyers for the fired business rep and two lawyers for the union employer, all in front of the judge, plus a U.S. lawyer from the union's American office.

During the less than one hour of testimony I sat in on, one witness was admitting to some, but not all, of the harmful sexual comments that were alleged. I kept picturing the clock ticking away for those five lawyers. If the union's management had taken the simplest of steps, they wouldn't have been in this mess playing out in court.

Tip #39 Look out for the legal bills

The average award in general damages in Canadian human rights cases is small, relative to other legal proceedings. Paying more than $5,000 would be considered a large award. The courts and tribunals consistently point out that since human rights legislation is meant to be remedial, not punitive, these awards for mental anguish, hurt feelings and humiliation, tend to be small.

To those who believe that the low dollar amounts fail to sufficiently discourage harassment, I say the process and legal

> Some of the biggest expenditures come from lost wages

costs are enough of a deterrent. Regardless, some of the biggest expenditures come from lost wages.

People don't stick around once they've filed a harassment complaint; they move to another workplace. They usually quit because management refused to do anything, or didn't do enough. Sadly, complainants are often so traumatized by their harassment, that they experience a psychological barrier to finding another job. Add to this the problem of explaining why they left their last job. "The boss sexually harassed me" or "I couldn't endure the poisoned environment that resulted from my colour of skin" or "I've filed a complaint with Human Rights" tends not to turn up on resumes.

If, during a human rights inquiry, tribunal or court case for wrongful dismissal, the company is found liable, the complainant will be asking for lost wages during the time he was out of a job. If there are extenuating circumstances, the mediator, adjudicator or judge will not award lost wages, but in all other cases, they will. Former employees are expected to look for new employment, but if they don't secure it immediately, the official considering their case will look at such criteria as the length of their employment, their age, the availability of similar jobs, and their state of mind as a result of the harassment they endured. I find that most adjudicators are conservative, awarding relatively small lost-wage settlements. Even so, it can cost the employer thousands of dollars-anywhere from four to twelve months of a salary. Since many wrongful dismissal cases involve supervisors and managers, that adds up.

Tip #40 Harassment prevention is cheaper

This is about risk management. It is simply far less costly to deal in-house with staff, than it will ever be to resolve a formal human rights complaint or wrongful dismissal court case. Yet sadly, most organizations don't adopt preventative measures; they wait until a crisis arises.

What are harassment's hidden costs?

Because we are conflict-adverse, we would usually rather not deal with harassment. People say: It's too stressful; not worth it; don't want to handle the fallout; I just took over and inherited this problem, etc. Although I've spelled out the many ways an organization can pay for a formalized harassment complaint, I haven't addressed the costs of avoiding harassment problems that don't end up in a formal process. Simply put, most businesses won't end up at a human rights commission, but if harassment is present, they're losing money left, right and centre.

One client of mine had a mid-sized company with a good work environment and friendly management. But harassment had turned up on their annual anonymous employee survey. Never mind that fewer than 10% of employees felt it was a problem; its very existence concerned management. As an employer of choice, they were surprised it was going on and wanted to correct it.

What does it take to be an employer of choice? I find these businesses pay their employees decently, but high salaries aren't what land them on the coveted list. They might not have gold-plated benefits, but the benefits are reasonable. As well, these businesses have a semblance of stability; they don't do layoffs at every sign of a downturn. Above all, however, employers of choice treat their employees with respect. And I mean real respect. Employers of choice deal with harassers immediately.

Tip #41 Unaddressed harassment costs money

Good employers know that dragging their feet on the issue will result in higher absenteeism and staff turnover, lower morale, and wasted time. All these translate to money, albeit money difficult to measure. All represent real costs that steal from the bottom line because harassed employees will spend time:

- Avoiding the harasser
- Stewing over what should have been said or done
- Plotting responses for the harasser
- Talking to colleagues about the problem
- Doubting their own abilities
- Blaming themselves

If the person being harassed perceives the manager to be slow at responding, the amount of time spent on the above will rise exponentially as you add in talking to colleagues about the errant supervisor as well as blaming the supervisor.

Time and again, when I have been called in to investigate harassment, I'm shocked by how long ago it occurred. If, for example, a racist remark was made two years earlier, the complainant can quote the time, day, exact location and people involved-sometimes even the weather and what people were wearing. But their most vivid memory of all is of the supervisor who could and should have addressed it promptly, saying nothing. When I talk to the supervisor, on the other hand, he typically can barely remember the situation, let alone any details. Or he remembers thinking it wasn't a big deal, that such things are said all the time, which is how he justified not getting involved.

I repeat: It was no big deal to the supervisor, but a lasting impression for the employee. And that supervisor expects employees to feel loyalty? Indeed, the employee not only lost respect for the supervisor, but for the company, because the "company" let a racist remark go unchallenged.

Parting tips for Harassment Headaches

Tip #42 Think beyond your own experience

Many a person is offended by something that does
not offend you. Anyone who fails to accept that is putting
his or her business at risk. Men don't always understand
what offends women and yet many times woman bite their
tongue when someone has crossed the line. Why don't they
speak up? They don't want a constant battle. But the more
it happens, the more likely a complaint will land you and
your business in trouble. The wise supervisor today lis-
tens-really listens-when employees who are of a different
gender, age, race, nationality or sexual orientation are willing to share what offends them. The very wisest solicit
such advice within an atmosphere that allows their colleagues to talk about it in comfort.

Tip #43 Don't do battle with definitions

Many a supervisor is bugged by today's definitions
of harassment, resents the liberal interpretations and
hates how easily management can be held responsible. If
you're among them, that's fine, but don't let it get in the
way of your business smarts-which tell you that unless
you can change the laws, you'd better adhere to them.
Even those with the influence to battle human rights legislation don't stand a chance with the Supreme Court of
Canada. And right now, members of the Supreme Court
aren't taking a lot of guff from legislatures withholding
basic protections to employees and citizens.

Tip #44 Be pro-active

Don't just stand there; do something! No need to
wait until a complaint starts traveling a formal road. When
someone tells a sexual joke, leap in. Say, "What did you
say?" in a forthright manner, or state, preferably within
hearing of other employees, "I don't want to hear jokes like
that in the future". You'd be amazed how such pro-active
comments will screech harassment to a stop, preventing

players from making more or larger mistakes. Whatever your style, you've go to do or say something.

Tip #45 Harassment-free is not fun-free

If you eliminate potential harassment from the workplace, have we choked out all the fun? How do you respond to those who whine, "Nowadays, you can't say anything!" I think we can still be fun, funny, provocative, interesting and even controversial, as long as we don't cross over the human rights line. Harassment prevention isn't about sterilizing the workplace. It's about extricating words or actions that are disrespectful. Don't worry; there are plenty of words, jokes and actions left over to smile and laugh about.

"Father, Mother, and Me,
Sister and Auntie say
All the people like us are We,
And everyone else is They.
And They live over the sea
While we live over the way,
But-would you believe it?-They look upon We
As only a sort of They!"
"We and They" by **Rudyard Kipling**

4

Treating "Different" People Differently

In the early 1980s, my sister Sharon participated in an exercise that examined the barriers Aboriginals face in their search for housing, as part of a university practicum process in Winnipeg. Two couples would go looking to rent an apartment-one couple Aboriginal, and the other (including my sister), non-Aboriginal. To keep the focus away from other issues, both couples were well-dressed and portrayed themselves as married, well educated (post-secondary) and professionals.

> Vacant apartments were unavailable to the Aboriginal couple, but available to the non-Aboriginal couple

Each spent a day visiting apartment buildings with vacancies, the Aboriginal couple always arriving first. Every time (with one exception), the Aboriginal couple was told the apartment was no longer available, while every time *without* exception, the non-Aboriginal couple was offered the apartment.

61

Even the Aboriginal participants in the study were surprised by the results. They let my sister know how dejected they felt by the blatancy of the discrimination. We need to remember that it's one thing to talk about discrimination, and a whole different matter to have it thrown in your face with such certainty.

Of course, that was the 1980s. How are Canadian Aboriginals doing today? When I ask people this question, even those who initially say we've come a long way end up admitting they're just hopeful of that.

Canadian research reinforces that persons who we refer to as "visible minorities" often have a rougher ride through life in this country. Take Toronto for example, our most diverse multicultural city. Our immigration department commissioned a report in 1997 that found Toronto displaying more racism than any other part of the country.[14] A 1998 study found that 10% of White and 56% of Black passengers disembarking from Air Canada flights from Jamaica got searched.[15] In a controversial series of articles and surveys done by the Toronto Star in 2002, Toronto Police documentation indicates that Blacks made up 23% of all arrests for criminal or drug offences, even though they comprise only 8% of the city's population.[16] And in December 2003, interviewing 400 people, the Ontario Human Rights Commission tabled a report outlining the harmful effects that racial profiling is having on persons, especially from the African Canadian, Arab, Chinese, South East Asian, Latin American, South Asian and Muslim communities.[17]

However, some people don't like statistics, so let me give you two recent examples involving Sikh Canadians. One involved an Indo-Canadian fellow who was walking with his wife and young children in the Vancouver area. Teenaged boys in a passing car threw a water balloon and it soaked him. The boys made some reference to his turban that was less than pleasant and sped away. This fellow didn't even have to use the word "humiliated" when he asked me, "What do you say to your children when this happens?"

The second example involves politics. I've been involved in the political process since I was nine. (My mother gave me a Stanfield sign at a Trudeau rally and sent me up front.) I've campaigned in Ontario, Manitoba, Saskatchewan, and British Columbia. I happen to be good at door to door canvassing and I've knocked on more doors than you can imagine. During a recent campaign in Vancouver, some friends of the candidate spent an afternoon canvassing door to door in a part of town with loads of apartments and condominiums. Upon their return, I asked how it went. They casually told me how they were hounded out of a few buildings, followed around in another and called names in the process. They didn't think this was a big deal at all, while I stood slack-jawed, listening to their stories.

Could it be coincidence that in all my years of canvassing, I rarely encountered the type of treatment they endured for an entire afternoon? I doubt it. I knew it had everything to do with the fact that they wore turbans.

What does this have to do with the workplace? The answer is simple and unfortunate. Being "different" in Canada's workforce today still involves barriers, many not readily identifiable.

Our own prejudices form the greatest barrier to creating an inclusive working environment. Prejudice means having pre-conceived ideas or pre-judging, and every one of us judges people before we know anything about them.

> The greatest barrier to creating an inclusive working environment stems from our own prejudices

To get beyond these barriers, we have to acknowledge that our own biases exist. Canada's Charter of Rights and Freedoms provides human rights protection in addition to the human rights legislation at the federal, provincial and territorial level. The federal and many provincial governments offer employment equity programs designed to "level the playing field". Though well-meaning, they are only as good as the level of buy-in among those who supervise people in the workplace.

When I first embarked on a career in human rights, I worried that I wasn't "pure" enough on this account. I knew I had deep-seated prejudices from being exposed to years of stereotyping. Eventually, I got over the notion that only the pure could operate in this arena. None of us is pure. But if we're smart, we learn to challenge ourselves, and to live within the law.

Stereotypes involve focusing on one, usually negative, characteristic of a person, then applying that to all others of a similar group. When women first started driving, it was common to hear the statement that women were bad drivers. Today, I frequently hear it said of Chinese drivers. I once had a Chinese woman tell me that it's not true all Chinese are bad drivers. She insisted only those from Mainland China, not from Hong Kong like herself, are bad drivers. It was a good lesson for me that stereotypes come from everyone and apply to all people.

Stereotypes get reinforced every day. My grandparents on my mother's side, Harriet and George McLean, came from Scotland, which gives me at least 50% Scottish heritage and all of us know the most common stereotype for Scots is "cheap". If we use this example, anytime you witness Scottish people being cheap, that picture stays in your mind. If a non-Scottish person is cheap, you might think "cheap b___", but since it doesn't fit your stereotype, you discard it and don't associate it as a defining characteristic of that person or his

> Stereotypes influence us to remember things that fit our established ideas and forget those that do not

ethnicity. You notice him, but you don't lump him in with a group based on any of his known characteristics. However, when you witness the same behaviour in a Scottish person, your mind automatically jumps to a conclusion based on your mind's defined picture of Scots being cheap. All of which leads you to swear on a stack of bibles, korans or torahs that all Scottish people are cheap; after all, you've seen it! And yes, I have my own cheap moments...

You don't think your mind works this way? Think back to the last time you bought a new car. Did you notice more of your new make of car on the road than usual as you drove it home? That's how filters-and stereotypes-work. We remember those things that fit our already established ideas and forget those that do not.

From a business perspective, stereotypes can have a huge impact. If we turn people down (for employment or promotions) based on negative stereotypes, and help others along due to positive stereotypes, we make it ever more difficult for ourselves to bury preconceived notions and allow the best people to shine.

The opposite of being ruled by stereotypes is building an inclusive workplace where people notice, value and learn from differences, but make an effort not to prejudge. It's not easy.

I find my own stereotypes come out worst when I'm bicycling to work. In a big city, cycling can be hazardous (not that it's always motorists' fault; I'm less than a saint in how I negotiate traffic). But when a driver cuts me off, I'm amazed at what goes through my head. If it's a woman, I'm thinking…well, you don't want to know. If it's someone visibly different than me, shocking words pop into my head. If it's some white guy, I might think, "jerk!", but most of my negative stereotypes are about people who don't look like me.

I'm sure I'm not alone. So when I hear people saying, "I don't have a prejudiced bone in my body," I let it slide for politeness' sake, but I don't believe it for a moment. Every person on this planet harbors some form of prejudice. We might not like to think we do, but we do.

Not having a "prejudiced bone" is right up there with being "colour blind". Even clinically colour-blind individuals notice a difference in skin colour. We all notice the skin colour of people around us; indeed, it would be insulting not to.

But how do we rid ourselves of stereotypes in order to create a business climate that promotes truly equal opportunities, good employee relations and impressive productivity?

Tip #46 Acknowledge your stereotypes

Rather than aspiring to rid yourself of stereotypes possibly embedded since childhood, it's better to acknowledge them, then aim at making sure your actions don't reflect what pops into your head. Here's an example: When I was doing my B.C. Bar Admission course in the late 1980s, I had a classmate I considered brilliant. Any firm would have been thrilled to have her, then or now. Yet here's a comment she encountered during a law firm interview: "We had one woman lawyer a few years ago and she didn't work out."

If one woman didn't work out, no women would work out? Try substituting "man" for the word "woman" and see how realistic that sounds.

If these same thoughts enter your head, train a red flag to pop up in your mind before you say it. Appeal to your rational side, and ask if the thought might involve stereotyping (don't crucify yourself for the thought as long as you squelched it before it became a comment).

Tip #47 Practical techniques compensate for stereotypes

Here's another constructive way to acknowledge your stereotypes and prejudices and pull others into your decision-making process when you are hiring, promoting or dealing generally with people. Where a single interview would normally make up your mind, resist letting that be the case, and have another staff member interview the candidates and share his or her opinions with you. This will surely increase the chances of logic prevailing over often unacknowledged

> To minimize prejudicial decisions, ensure that the decision-making team reflects a mix

prejudices. Finally, since so many of us do share these prejudices, it's important today for the decision-making team to reflect as much variety as possible. A gender and ethnic mix will increase the chances of objectivity. Different perspectives are healthy.

I've said that it's more important to acknowledge prejudice than pretend you can banish all internal prejudices. But that's not to say you can't or shouldn't try for an arbitrary change of mindset or behaviour. It's easier than you think. I've managed to moderate a lifetime of bad eating habits through a couple of tricks. I always used to snack in the evening, and I'm not talking carrots and apples, but potato chips and peanuts. I was known to sit down in front of the television with a jar of peanut butter in my lap and a bag of crackers beside me. It followed with the guilt as I went to bed, a restless night of sleep, and that oh, so painful experience in the morning-getting on the scale in front of the mirror. I didn't want to look at myself (let alone the scale). Logically, I knew this was bad, and that I should be able to resist indulging in such a routine. But I didn't lick the habit by self-discipline. I employed two tricks: banishing chips and peanuts from my home, and brushing my teeth after supper (because I never eat after I brush my teeth). Pathetic? Maybe. But it worked, so who cares.

Let's get away from the topic of food (which is making me hungry) and get back to the issue of attempting to override stereotypes. One example of how I've managed to change arbitrary behaviour relates to people butting into line at a bus stop or at the grocery counter. Having a strong sense of fair play, I'm often inclined to tell them (politely) to get to the back of the line. Similarly, if I see someone being rude, or smoking in a no-smoking zone, I'm burning to speak up. However, one day I noticed that I was making more comments to easier targets; a young student or someone not as big as me. With the demographic make-up of the Vancouver area, often these people were of a different ethnic make-up than mine, although by no means exclusively. This raised a flag for me, forced me to think.

Now I adhere to a new rule. I'll only say something to a person if I'd say the same thing to a line backer for the B.C. Lions. If I wouldn't, then I leave them alone. Just like the late night snacking, I'm using a practical technique to change my behaviour to get a better result.

Tip #48 Accept your stereotypes – just don't act on them

My point is that I think we should accept that we pick up stereotypes and we prejudge people all the time. But we don't have to act on our stereotypes. If we had the "thought police", I'm sure they'd condemn me to capital punishment for some of my thoughts. But it's not our thoughts that matter as long as our behaviour reflects giving people the best opportunities they have coming to them. That sense of fairness will get you the best employees and will enhance morale.

When we make business and organizational decisions based on stereotypes and prejudices, we miss out on a number of different fronts. For example:

- *Losing out on good candidates.* If you think that certain people will be consistently late, lazy, or unreliable, based on stereotypes, you'll let good people slip through your fingers. My first job in "personnel" with a major retailer had me looking for an employee for a high-end women's fashion department. I found the perfect candidate. She was knowledgeable about the merchandise, friendly, and had good retail experience. Lucky for her, Manitoba had strict rules about application forms, so I didn't know she was only 18 years old until I had given her the job and she had to fill out pertinent information. I said then, and I knew it to be true, that if I had known her age, I would never have given her the job. I had it in my mind that we needed someone older.

- *Letting stereotypes determine bad people.* Many a political and social commentator has concluded that Aboriginals and Black Canadians are more involved in crime, based on the fact that they're over-represented in Canadian jails. A retail employee who subscribes to this notion will have a hard time not hovering over Aboriginal and Black customers every time they walk through the door. If this same employee is less inclined to watch White customers as closely, who are they going to catch shoplifting more often, and will that not confirm their stereotype? At the same time, who gets to walk out of the store undetected? And so the cycle continues.

- *Assuming that positive stereotypes are a good thing.* Anyone who thinks that negative stereotyping is bad and positive stereotyping is good should ask a Chinese adult who was always lousy at math or a Jewish person with poor business instincts what that was like. So-called "positive" stereotypes set up unrealistic expectations that are difficult to fulfill. Hiring people based on positive stereotypes is no better for your workplace's bottom line than letting negative stereotypes influence decisions. Qualifications and abilities are all you need to search for.

Never mind the laws and policies in our country; the truly most effective way to break down barriers and attract the best and most productive workers is to acknowledge our prejudices, then try to overcome them.

Differences and Discomfort

We've accepted that we have certain stereotypes and we've decided to try and reduce their impact. That gives us confidence in finding the right employees and customers and treating them fairly. But it doesn't always negate the fact that sometimes we're not sure what to say or do around people who are different from us and with whom we haven't grown up. Despite progress at integration within Canada, the majority of people still befriend, marry and partner with people who look and act like they do.

We do this partly because it keeps us in our comfort zone. If someone makes us feel uncomfortable, we often fail to give that person a fair chance, justifying this on the sense that it's not "the right fit". In the workplace, that discomfort can stem from someone having a different language or culture, or having different physical or mental abilities.

Language

It's not uncommon for English speakers to think that people who don't speak English as a first language are not as smart. A part of us knows it's ridiculous, but how many people do we pass over before we face this inner prejudice?

> Do you avoid people in an attempt to limit episodes of embarrassing communication?

All of us have strange notions related to language. Have you ever caught yourself raising your voice when speaking to someone who has trouble with English? If you feel forced to say, "Could you repeat that" too many times, do you avoid that person in an attempt to limit episodes of embarrassing communication attempts?

Differences in culture can lead to the same sort of discomfort. We become afraid to make comments or ask certain questions for fear of embarrassing another person or ourselves. Instead of asking questions or taking the risk of offending, we take the easy way out by surrounding ourselves with people much like us. That way, there's no risk and everyone feels comfortable.

This is not a phenomenon restricted to English-speaking White people of European descent. It's second nature to most humans. In September 2003, Statistics Canada released the results of a study that tracked the destination patterns of new immigrants to Canada. In the three largest metropolitan areas - Toronto, Montreal and Vancouver - 44% of highly skilled immigrants indicated they chose their city on the basis of being close to family and friends. Only 19% chose their destination according to job prospects. I believe this indicates that living in our comfort zone and having support is more important than pursuing career ambitions.

Disabilities

It can be uncomfortable for the able-bodied to interact with people who have physical or mental disabilities. We don't know how to act. Don't believe that? Talk to a person in a wheelchair; any can tell you of bizarre behaviours they've observed from able-bodied people. One of the most common is when they are chatting with an able-bodied person, and a third person joins the conversation. If the third person is able-bodied, often the dialogue will only be carried on with the other able-bodied person, sometimes even referring to the person in the wheelchair as if he or she isn't there.

For four years, I was on the board of directors of the Western Institute for the Deaf and Hard of Hearing. I wanted to do community service work, and I thought this was a perfect fit because my dad has been hard of hearing since birth. But even after four years of talking and debating with deaf people, I still feel a level of uncertainty when I'm alone with a deaf person and have no translator. Strangely, I always feel the deaf person is responsible for putting me at ease. If he or she doesn't, I don't seem to know what to do. I learned so much during those four years and yet one great lesson came from understanding why deaf people want to continue to communicate in their own language, instead of trying to fit into the hearing world. When deaf people communicate with one another, they experience much more comfort.

If I learned anything in those four years, it's that levels of comfort run both ways. Many deaf people prefer spending time with one another versus trying to fit into the hearing world.

Here's an exercise I sometimes include in workplace training sessions. I ask, "If you were to have a disability or disorder, which of the following would you choose?"

- Deafness
- Blindness
- Being a paraplegic (paralysis of legs)
- Having a learning disability

Most people choose deafness because they perceive that it will hinder their life the least. Then I ask them what type of person they'd hire, if they were to integrate more persons with disabilities into their workforce. Very few choose to work with a deaf person. Most opt for the person who is paraplegic. Why? Because we prefer to interact with a hearing person to avoid communication problems.

Tip #49 Discomfort shouldn't interfere with business

Why are we so hung up on having only comfortable communication? I don't know, but when Helen Keller was asked which was more difficult, being deaf or being blind, she replied: "Blindness cuts a person off from things, but deafness cuts a person off from people." Employers need to ensure that merely feeling uncomfortable isn't an excuse for inadvertently cutting people off from otherwise stellar workers. At the least, it may encourage a valuable employee to leave your employ and seek another.

When it comes to discomfort due to language, culture or disabilities, try to deal with it. It's better to risk discomfort by asking a person to repeat something you don't understand. Likewise, if you're not certain what to say or do around people with disabilities, feel free to ask questions. If you ask in a respectful manner, most people will be happy to help you out; it's usually not their first time.

Kid-Gloves

In the early 1980s, the vice president of human resources at a large Canadian company was describing to me a problem with one of his employees. He finished off his input with the sarcastic comment, "And the best part of all, she's black." I knew what he meant by that and what he was thinking - if they didn't handle the situation properly, she was more than likely to file a complaint of discrimination. I call this the "kid-glove" syndrome; many a worker feels that a fellow employee who is a member of a minority group (or female) needs or gets special (extra gentle) treatment either in an effort to protect them or as a way of avoiding a human rights complaint.

Tip #50 Don't use kid-gloves

We don't do anyone any favors by treating people with kid-gloves. It's a disservice and adds fuel to the fire of those who aspire to keep anyone out who is considered different.

First, it's insulting to a person in a minority to be offered special treatment when none is needed. Second, it creates resentment from other employees. Third, it leads employers to avoid hiring other people who are different. They fall back on how the last woman or Sikh man lead to perceived problems.

Enforce rules, correct behaviour, and dish out discipline evenly; everyone should get fair treatment. If employees come to you saying they feel they're being treated more harshly than another due to their gender or ethnicity, listen carefully in case there is something to it. If you've done your job properly, your explanation will go a long way to correcting the misconception or misunderstanding.

Tip #51 Listen carefully to a complaint of discrimination

Ever since the O.J. Simpson trial, people talk about someone playing the "race card", or eliciting sympathy because they're in a victim role. Despite this, I'd advise you to not dismiss out of hand a person who thinks he or she is being victimized due to gender, religion, sexual orientation or such. If you've never been in those shoes, it's all too easy to dismiss their view. As a company leader, you've been entrusted to listen and weigh such judgments carefully.

In 1977 at the University of Manitoba, I was in a large class with a friend, Mark, who sat a couple of seats over. I was more interested in fun than academia that year; during this first year I was more or less concentrating on a "major in beverages". And I was forever looking over at Mark and making strange faces to distract him. At the end of this class, a Black student who sat between Mark and me asked, "Why do you keep staring at me?" I was stunned and explained that I'd been trying to get Mark's attention. Although he seemed satisfied with that, I remember thinking he was making something out of nothing.

Looking back, and keeping in mind that this was the late 1970s in Winnipeg, when there were a limited number of Black students at the University, I realize this classmate probably got more than his share of people staring at him. This fellow did the right thing, asking me to explain my behaviour rather than making an assumption. Had I been staring at him, he would have had every right to ask me to stop.

As with that situation, in your workplace, your actions as a supervisor or manager speak louder than words. If your decisions are fair and equitable, you're less likely to be visited by an employee who feels that he or she is being singled out by you for mistreatment. In fact, you'll be a more effective leader as employees will know you are fair to everyone.

Does it seem to you that I'm speaking out of both sides of my mouth? On the one hand, I'm saying don't treat people with kid gloves for fear they might cry sexism or racism. And on the other hand, I'm saying listen carefully if a person says they're being singled out due to sexism or racism. Until we get closer to a society where people base their decisions on a rational basis and not so much on prejudices, we will have these complexities. My point is, don't worry about the times a misunderstanding happens. Treat people equitably, explain rationally, and most of the time, people will respond reasonably. We certainly don't achieve perfection by hiring only people who look like us, so we shouldn't expect perfection from a mixed gender and multicultural workforce.

Parting tips for Treating "Different" People Differently

Tip #52 Challenge stereotypes

When someone makes a comment that reflects stereotyping, you can make a big difference at work by challenging that assumption. You don't have to make a big deal out of it, but you'd be wise not to let it go unchallenged. This does two things: It lets that person know she doesn't have an audience with you on this and other stereotypes, and it lets others at work know you don't support harmful stereotypes.

Tip #53 Don't waste time fighting old battles

When you find yourself arguing in the workplace for banning turbans in the RCMP or urging immigrants to adopt Western religions, it's time to stop arguing-at least at work. Whether or not you agree with views that contradict current human rights legislation, don't get sucked into expressing those views at work if you and your business want to prosper in our multicultural country. Many longstanding notions are based on stereotypes, but there's no sign our country is moving back towards supporting them, legally or otherwise.

Tip #54 Act; don't just react

If some of the issues raised in this chapter are interfering with you getting the best candidates and opportunities, be willing to get pro-active. You don't have to wait until an employee exit interview, when someone complains or tells you things are rotten. Many of these issues cause us discomfort because we think we shouldn't notice differences and we think no one has prejudices. It's like the adage of an elephant being in a room, but no one wants to talk about it. If an elephant has been in your office for a while, be willing to stand up and say, "we have an elephant in our office-can we talk about this?" More to the point, if stereotyping or discrimination is obvious in your business, find some way of addressing these issues. If leaders are willing to be open about problems or potential problems, you've got a much better chance of employees speaking up. Often we don't want to rock the boat by talking about sensitive topics. It's a lot better to rock the boat than watch it sink slowly.

"I believe in equality for everyone, except reporters and photographers."

Mohandas Gandhi

5
Inclusiveness, Not Affirmative Action

In November of 1993, the Government of Ontario advertised a senior management position paying between $74,000 and $111,000 (for a director of information). Nice job, and nothing unusual - except that the posting stated it was available only to persons with disabilities, Aboriginals, women, francophones or visible minorities. In other words, no able-bodied, white, English-speaking men need apply. Only a few days transpired before Ontario Premier Bob Rae intervened. Voila! The restrictions on the job qualifications disappeared, and a review of policy went into motion.

Almost ten years later, the federal government posted a senior management job for the Department of Fisheries with similar restrictions. Though it drew attention, it never got withdrawn. I don't think Canadians have changed their opinion about excluding people from job opportunities, but maybe we're more resigned to the process.

Even so, these types of job exclusions are few and far between in Canada. You'll find more in the United States under various forms of affirmative action. And yet, ask a typical Canadian if such exclusions are prevalent, and you'll learn that many believe so. Unfortunately, this false belief is preventing business people from taking advantage of opportunities to have employees and clients reflect the communities in which we live and work.

It isn't necessary for Canadian businesses to go as far as adopting what most people think of as affirmative action, or quotas. As long as there are no hidden, perceived or real barriers to employment or services, there is no problem. Only when prejudice and stereotyping result in discrimination do governments step in to regulate equity and fairness so that every citizen has equal access to the same opportunities. Therefore, programs have been created in an attempt to redress discrimination in employment. I think it's important that business leaders know the Canadian as well as American requirements so that they understand the reasoning for equity programs and realize the business benefits.

Affirmative Action in the United States

Despite the fact that the American civil war saw an end to slavery, many African Americans, not just in the South, were denied basic rights into the 1960s and 1970s, leading to the civil rights movement and resulting historical changes to the law. Affirmative action grew out of a desire to achieve equality of results, not just equality of opportunity. As controversial as it was, authorities saw bussing students from one part of town to another as the only way to ensure equal access to proper education. To get this result, the U.S. Supreme Court overturned its earlier "separate but equal" doctrine, which allowed for separation of Blacks and Whites where circumstances were deemed equal. In the groundbreaking *Brown v. Board of Education* decision of 1954, Chief Justice Earl Warren noted that separate but equal was "inherently unequal". The response: School boards voluntarily accepted bussing programs, or courts imposed them. Parents, administrators and judges began grappling with how to achieve real equality, not just laws written on paper.

The same held true for employment. While the fourteenth amendment of the U.S. constitution guaranteed equal protection under the law, getting real equality often proved elusive. In 1965 at a commencement address at Howard University, President Lyndon B. Johnson spoke of the need for "equality as a result", not just equality of opportunity. He said:

> *You do not take a person who for years, has been hobbled by chains, and liberate him, bring him up to the starting line of a race and then say, 'You are free to compete with all the others,' and still justly believe that you have been completely fair.*

President Johnson issued executive orders to provide equal opportunities in federal employment, first based on race, creed, colour or national origin, and then two years later, added gender to the list. President Richard Nixon went further, with executive orders to include affirmative action plans on any contractors doing business with the government. These contractors were to correct any employment "deficiencies" regarding minorities and women with a system not of "rigid and inflexible quotas", but of reasonably attainable "targets". Thus continued President Johnson's goal of attaining "equality as a result".

Employment Equity in Canada

In Canada, the federal government was looking to examine its own employment deficiencies around June 1983, when then-Employment Minister Lloyd Axworthy created a Royal Commission with Ontario Judge Rosalie Abella at the helm. (Abella went on to become a Supreme Court of Canada Justice.) Judge Abella was to "inquire into the most efficient, effective, and equitable means of promoting equal employment opportunities" in Canada. The result? An examination of eleven federal crown corporations and corporations wholly owned by the government of Canada. Coincidentally, many of these eleven, which employed some 175,000, are today private corporations. They include Petro-Canada, Air Canada, Canadian National Railway, Canada Mortgage and Housing Corporation, Canada Post, Canadian Broadcasting

Corporation, Atomic Energy of Canada Limited, Export Development Corporation, Teleglobe Canada, The de Havilland Aircraft of Canada Limited, and the Federal Business Development Bank.

In October 1984, when Abella presented her findings to the government in a report entitled "Equality in Employment", she outlined the wide-ranging and systemic problems facing many Canadians looking for equal employment opportunities.

If...we are not always sure what 'equality' means, most of us have a good understanding of what is 'fair.' And what is happening today in Canada to women, native people, disabled persons, and visible minorities is not fair. It is not fair that many people in these groups have restricted employment opportunities, limited access to decision-making processes that critically affect them, little public visibility as contributing Canadians, and a circumscribed range of options generally. It may be understandable, given history, culture, economics, and even human nature, but by no standard is it fair.

She defined the obstacles as higher unemployment, higher over-qualification, occupational segregation, lower wages and limited opportunities for promotions, noting that overall, the problem was "systemic".

To begin correcting these systemic inequities, Abella proposed that employers concentrate on breaking down barriers that get in the way of true employment opportunities, rather than trying to fill job quotas. She urged employers to examine how they recruit, train, evaluate, advance and even lay off employees. She directed them to look at their pay, benefits, and all components of operation to uncover barriers to the designated groups.

It is not that individuals in the [employment equity] designated groups are inherently unable to achieve equality on their own; it is that the obstacles in their way are so formidable and self-perpetuating that they cannot be overcome without intervention.

Less than two years later, the federal government announced the Federal Employment Equity Act (which covered federally regulated companies with one hundred employees or more), a Federal Contractors program, and an employment equity policy. Since then, the federal government has reinforced and enacted new legislation to ensure that the principles of employment equity continue. These programs mean that if your business falls under federal jurisdiction (banks, airlines, etc.) or you have a sizable contract with the federal government, you have to show the government that you are an equal opportunity employer and have actual programs in place to prove that the policy is more than mere words.

How does this relate to your business if you are not covered by federal regulation? Depending on your provincial, territorial or municipal jurisdiction, you may have employment equity requirements of your own. If you don't, all Canadians, including employers, must abide by the requirements of a human rights act or code, and these often spell out or allow for programs equivalent to employment equity. In other words, even if your provincial human rights code does not force you to have employment equity programs, it may allow you to do so voluntarily. This is also true with the Canadian Charter of Rights and Freedoms.

Hence, employment equity is meant to level the playing field, and when the playing field is too uneven, employers are allowed to create special programs that can deal with past or present wrongs. For example, an employer can set up a special recruitment drive encouraging women to apply for work in a male dominaed workplace. All women would still have to meet the needed criteria, but the employer would spend some time seeking out women to apply. Another example is creating a mentor program for Aboriginal employees already on the job, as a way of assisting them in keeping their jobs, and making sure they don't receive negative attention based on stereotypes.

Lots of people regard these types of special programs as reasonable, but many more consider them unfair interventionist programs, and that gets their goat. Even where we believe in equal opportunities, most of us have difficulty understanding how severe the barriers are for people traditionally outside the mainstream employment process. So inevitably, some look at employment equity programs as favouring designated groups rather than leveling the playing field.

If I had a dollar for every time someone told me there were massive quota systems going on in Canada, I'd be writing this book from my beachfront mansion in Tahiti. Yes, there are cases where people actively make spaces available for people in designated groups. But more often, there is nothing even resembling a quota system at work. After a few people have sworn on their mother's grave that "x" organization is not hiring white males, I called up to find the real story. I discovered each time that either it was greatly exaggerated, or there was no truth at all to such rumours.

Here's an example. Often people tell me there is a hiring freeze for white males in the RCMP. The reality is that there is a strong push to recruit Aboriginal Canadians, in hopes they'll address crime and crime prevention within Canada's fastest growing population group. The RCMP holds open a number of places while recruiting Aboriginals, but in the end, after they've hired officers who meet the necessary criteria, Aboriginals make up a small percentage of the officers hired. Most new RCMP officers look a lot like me: white male (except they're younger and in better shape). The reality is a long way from the perception that white males need not apply.

When there is a quota system, its existence stems from years of human rights neglect that the tribunals and courts will no longer tolerate. For example, in 1987 women made up 13% of employees in non-traditional jobs, while at the Canadian National Railway (CNR), it was only 0.7%.

Years earlier, the Quebec group, Action Travail des Femmes complained to the Federal Human Rights

Commission, stating that CNR was discriminating against women in their hiring and promotion practices. The Commission set up a Human Rights Tribunal to consider a "class" complaint after 155 complaints had been lodged against CNR by February of 1982. When proceeding to the Supreme Court of Canada, then-Chief Justice Brian Dixon maintained that evidence clearly established that Canadian National's recruitment, hiring and promotion policies "prevented and discouraged women from working on blue collar jobs".

In fact, CNR's pattern of discrimination against women was widespread. Women were:

- Virtually excluded from the out-reach recruitment programs
- Not given information about filling nontraditional positions
- Strongly discouraged from applying for nontraditional jobs, and strongly encouraged to apply for secretarial jobs
- Not told clearly the qualifications needed to fill certain jobs
- Required to take physical tests of strength that no man was asked to take
- Expected to have welding experience for jobs where no welding took place
- Subjected to sexual harassment and comments that implied they were taking work away from men

Therefore in 1987, the Supreme Court of Canada upheld a decision of the Canadian Human Rights Tribunal, ordering CNR to hire one woman for every four non-traditional jobs filled until they got to the national average of women in non-traditional jobs in Canada.[18]

The federal Human Rights Commission and the Supreme Court of Canada wanted to ensure women were given the same opportunities as men at CNR. Yet, this case is often misunderstood or misstated with many Canadians thinking CNR was forced into an affirmative action program to hire women or to give them preferential treatment for some kind of politically correct experiment. Instead, this decision was designed to correct the outrageous discrimination women had faced for decades. As Dixon emphasized, the program was "designed to break a continuing cycle of systemic discrimination" and to "ensure that future applicants and workers from the affected group will not face the same insidious barriers".

Why is this information important, and why should it concern your business? After all, few people openly support discriminatory practices. Does it really matter that not everyone gets the job he or she wants, or that some people are segregated into certain jobs? Employment equity might be a lofty goal, but is it my business?

Tip #55 Reflecting your community is great for business

Beyond the human rights reasons, making sure your business or department better reflects the community you serve is good, in fact, great for business.

Here's why:

Decisions will not be made in a vacuum. When decisions are made with only persons from the same or similar backgrounds, important components are often missing. Take something as simple as setting dates for a meeting, a big sale or the opening of a new location. Even with a decent day-timer or calendar, which lists a variety of important celebrations and holy days, if you don't understand the significance of certain holidays in certain cultures, how will you know a good time to set an important meeting you want everyone to attend?

Which of the following dates should you avoid when setting up a fall meeting?

- Labour Day
- Rosh Hashanah
- Yom Kippur
- Diwali
- Remembrance Day
- Eid al-Fitr
- Christmas Day

If you were brought up in a home like mine, you have no clue about four of the above. In fact, I only know about Rosh Hashanah and Yom Kippur because I attended York University, which shut down for three days every fall. Given my law-school reading load, I was eternally grateful to my Jewish classmates for "giving" me those days off to catch up or lounge. They replied it was payback time for all those Christmases they'd enjoyed off. Rosh Hashanah is a two-day event (one day for Reform Jews) for celebrating the New Year. Yom Kippur, the Day of Atonement, is the holiest day of the year for Jews.

I've come to understand the importance of Diwali, the Hindu "Festival of Lights", as a result of living in the Lower Mainland of B.C., marked by a large Indo-Canadian population. As for Eid al-Fitr, I had to call a Muslim friend and ask for advice. I knew the importance of the month-long fasting and praying of Ramadan, but I didn't truly appreciate the importance of its last day. On this day, many Muslims seek a day off work to eat, visit with friends and celebrate.

There are so many customs, procedures and even superstitions in every culture, that it's impossible to keep track of them all. But when you have a workplace that reflects the community you serve, there is a better chance someone will give you important information to make sure you're not alienating a large customer base or missing out on a business opportunity.

> When your workplace reflects the community you serve, you stand a better chance of leveraging opportunities and avoiding problems

When your workplace reflects the community you serve, you stand a better chance of leveraging opportunities and avoiding problems.

Customers want to see themselves reflected in business and government. Years ago, as part of a large project for a company, I did an audit of their practices with an eye to encouraging and supporting diversity. It soon dawned on me that the firm's customer base looked a lot different from their workforce. Most workers were white, while visible minorities comprised much of their customer base. Their employees noticed this and increasingly so did their customers. They were surprised to find that their paper policies of supporting diversity were not reflected in their hiring and promotion practices.

Your customers aren't stupid. If they look around your business and notice it's homogenous while the community and customer base is diverse, they'll notice. If they have an alternative supplier, they'll use it. If there isn't, it leads to a perfect business opportunity to compete against you.

However, a word of caution on the issue of reflecting the community. Don't let tokenism be your guide. In the audit noted above, any visible minority employees often found visible minority customers sent directly to them, with no allowance made for whether they were busy or had the expertise to help that customer. Don't let this happen. If visible minority customers need special attention based on their ethnicity, they'll let you know.

Avoiding the "us versus them" mentality. When your business reflects your community - when you achieve a critical mass of people from different backgrounds- employees and customers will stop suspecting "tokenism" (people hired to fill quotas), and start realizing you have hired people in a competitive employment market with competent people everywhere.

Tip #56 The public will take action if you don't

Nowadays, the consumer plays a much bigger role than government regulation. That is, customers who feel they've been discriminated against by a business are more likely to take matters into their own hands by speaking loudly with their wallets and telling friends or the media. Very few will file a human rights complaint. Instead, if people don't see themselves reflected in a business, they'll go elsewhere if they have the option.

And when the public deals with government as a service provider, individually or through member organizations, people will ask elected officials to force changes to ensure that government employees reflect the community in which they serve. For example, when there are not enough women or Chinese Canadian police officers, the public will more likely demand changes from a city councilor than they will take their case to a human rights commission.

To avoid this dilemma, break down barriers and actively encourage all people to apply. Soon you'll achieve the diversity for which people are looking. Here are a few examples where businesses could have done a better job reflecting the community and therefore avoided damaging publicity.

Tip #57 Include and listen to people different from you

Aviation

In March of 1992, Canadian Airlines International booking agent Billie Mortimer revealed publicly that Japan Airlines (JAL) had a practice of seating South Asians at the back of their planes. This surfaced because JAL had sub-contracted Canadian Airlines to be their booking agent in Vancouver, and the 50 Canadian staff involved were being pressed to carry out this discriminatory practice. JAL responded by justifying the practice. Most of the Indian passengers, officials argued, were migratory farm workers and their families, and because they spoke little English, didn't smoke and required meatless meals, they were better served as a group. Mortimer, however, contends that she was told other passengers were offended by their odour.

JAL changed its segregationist practices a few weeks later when British Columbia Indian, multicultural and anti-racism groups garnered national media attention by calling for a boycott of JAL. The groups were in the process of contacting people in other parts of the world to extend the boycott beyond B.C.'s borders when JAL made the change.

Think of the bad publicity and revenue loss both JAL and Canadian could have avoided if Indo-Canadian employees had been involved in setting policy.

Sports

On June 29, 2001, the United States Supreme Court ruled that professional golfer Casey Martin, due to a circulatory disorder in his right leg, could use a golf cart at Professional Golfers' Association tournaments even though other professional golfers could not. This controversial decision was debated far and wide in the golf world. My dad, an ardent golfer, had talked about it ever since Martin first launched his lawsuit in 1997. It came as a surprise, then, when caddie Les Leonhardt was told at an Ontario Golf Association (OGA) tournament a week later that he couldn't use a power cart to caddie for his friend Vince Dwyer.

Dwyer, with a three handicap (for you non-golfers, that's phenomenal), was in a qualifying tournament with the Ontario Golf Association (now the Golf Association of Ontario, GAO) in June 2001. The top eight golfers would represent their district and allow them to compete at the provincial level, the Canadian level, and possibly represent our country internationally in amateur golf. Many golfers at the top of their game in this amateur stream go on to become professional golfers.

When Dwyer's normal caddie was injured the week before, he asked Leonhardt to be his caddie. Leonhardt has a partially amputated leg and wears a prosthesis. On the morning of the tournament both men secured permission from two registration officials for Leonhardt to use the cart as a caddie, with strict instructions that Dwyer could not sit in the cart at any time.

According to Dwyer and Leonhardt, after they'd played the first hole and were preparing to tee off at the second, an OGA official drove up in a power cart to tell Dwyer that he was disqualified from the qualification part of the tournament, although he could continue playing the round of golf. They exchanged a few words and Dwyer

87

continued with his game, but both he and Leonhardt noted how badly he played until he calmed down. In the end, Dwyer tied for 11th place, outside of the top eight to qualify for the 2001 year.

I spoke to Vince Dwyer and Les Leonhardt about this issue. More than two years after the fact, Dwyer was still incensed over what happened to his friend. "It was absolutely humiliating," he told me. "When people's feelings are affected, that can be for life." Leonhardt will have nothing more to do with the GAO, even though he still golfs four or five times a week with a seven handicap. (When Leonhardt golfs, he uses a power cart on the course to get to the ball, but gets out of the cart to hit the ball.) What bothers Leonhardt and Dwyer most is that they never received an apology. Dwyer wanted to take this case to the Ontario Human Rights Commission, but after speaking to two lawyers, decided not to pursue it.

The OGA's problems did not stop with two men being upset. For more than a week, the local, then national press ran with the story. During a Kitchener, Ontario phone-in radio show, the public was less than kind to the OGA.

Both the Ontario and Canadian golf associations allow for the use of power carts in seniors' tournaments, and where the golfer has a disability. Associations wisely ask for medical evidence of the disability before making a final determination. The reason the rules are strict is to ensure that one golfer is not enjoying an edge when other golfers have to walk the course. However, last I checked, the associations still had no stated policy on caddies using a power cart.

My point is that businesses of all kinds need to be proactive around issues of disabilities, especially as our population ages. Why wait to respond to negative headlines and embarrassing radio talk shows when such issues are easily anticipated if we think proactively and include more than just able-bodied decision-makers in our midst?

Military

Even at the highest reaches of world government and military, mistakes happen. In September 2001, after the attacks on New York's World Trade Centre and the Pentagon, the United States government was trying to create a broad based coalition to fight terrorism. The Pentagon's initial name for the military response to the Taliban regime in Afghanistan and their support of Al Qaeda terrorists, was called "Operation Infinite Justice". However, several Islamic scholars immediately objected to the name, U.S. Defence Secretary Donald Rumsfeld was told, because only God, or Allah, will determine infinite justice.

Because it was clearly in the best interest of the United States to get American and foreign Muslims on-side, the offensive was renamed "Operation Enduring Freedom". This name had no religious connotations to it and therefore could not be seen as a religious lightning rod when the focus was to unite people to fight terrorism and the Taliban government.

Like the military, business leaders need to be both sensitive to issues, and inclusive. The Pentagon wasted time and resources, risked alienating people, for not doing their homework up front. All they needed to do was float the proposed name by a variety of people from different backgrounds and beliefs.

Tip #58 Reach out to attract a variety of employees

Ok, so I understand the business positives for reflecting the communities my business serves. But for some reason, I'm not getting the diversity of candidates knocking on my door. Valid point.

When you tend to get applicants who look like you, or more importantly don't look like your community, this begs the question, why are certain people staying away? Let's look at the police force as an example. Most Canadians approach the police expecting safety and trust. However, police forces in some countries are known for their corruption; there is very little trust. Hence, it doesn't occur to many Canadian immigrants and refugees to seek Canadian police for assistance, let alone to apply for a career with the force. Police throughout Canada have been actively working with multicultural and social service agencies for years to rectify this situation. As a result, Canadian police forces are starting to better reflect the population and are therefore making it easier to work with communities who otherwise are suspicious of them.

If you're not in the policing business, maybe you're not as worried about trust, yet you might have to do a type of outreach similar to that of the police. Outreach involves making contact with people with whom you don't typically spend time. However, don't feel you have to do it alone. If your business belongs to an association, find out what outreach efforts they have made. You may find resources and contacts already available. If not, be proactive and start an outreach program that will benefit your organization and others of interest. An outreach program can involve getting to know more about a group of people, or it can be as simple as sponsoring an event or placing ads in community or ethnic-specific papers. You don't have to rush in; building relationships takes time.

There may be times when you decide trust in your business *is* an issue. In those cases customers avoid shopping at-or applying to-businesses due to a reputation that people of their ethnicity are not treated well. Based on truth or not, outdated or current, a negative reputation is difficult to dispel. Most owners, managers, and employees would love to know if something is keeping customers and applicants away, so they can correct the problem. If you hear even a trace of this for your business, you'll need to rectify it or your business will suffer.

Systemic Discrimination

If your workplace doesn't accurately reflect the population (don't worry, no one is looking for an exact replica), it doesn't necessarily mean that you're doing something terribly wrong. However, double-check whether your employment and business practices might involve direct or inadvertent discrimination or harassment. Ensure your policies and practices do not have systemic barriers working in favour of some and against others. And work hard at letting people know you are friendly and open to all employees and customers. If you are vigilant in these and other areas, you may never have to take interventionist action. But beware. Systemic discrimination is rarely something you can point your finger at and say, "Aha, this is where we're going wrong."

> Systemic discrimination is rarely something you can point your finger at and say, "Aha, this is where we're going wrong."

Tip #59 Do an audit of your business

Businesses should take time to ensure they are truly inclusive, through either critical analysis, an audit of the workplace or both. If you conduct a formal audit, be prepared for some boat rocking as employees are asked to be critical of strategies that have always worked for them (or you) in the past.

- What types of applicants do you tend to attract? Is there diversity among potential hires? Could hiring from referrals be perpetuating the problem?
- Do employees and supervisors know the basics of workplace human rights issues and the importance of accommodating differences?
- Who are your clients? If your business exists in a multicultural community, but that's not your client base, what changes could you make to attract a broader base of clients?
- What does your physical space say to clients and employees? Do the pictures or paintings on your wall reflect the breadth of your community?
- When employees leave, do you know why? Do you have an anonymous exit-interviewing process to prevent employment mistakes from repeating themselves?

Take time to look over your workplace objectively. Being inclusive is not about affirmative action. It is sound business practice. Today's immigrants are no longer from predominantly white, English-speaking countries. The Aboriginal population is the fastest growing in the country. Women have entered the workforce in large numbers, and persons with disabilities are winning court cases left and right as they insist on basic rights and dignity that for years had been denied them. Individuals with minority religious beliefs are also winning cases in court. The more your organization reflects the population it serves, the better chance you have of enhancing your business and casting a wider net for more clients.

Parting Tips for Inclusiveness, Not Affirmative Action

Tip #60 Fight notions of tokenism

If you start new hiring patterns, deal right away with any notions that this is affirmative action or tokenism. Beware of the "revolving door" employment-equity syndrome, where you do a great job hiring minority candidates, but not keeping them. Is the workplace climate conducive to retaining such new talent? A bad workplace climate might include more than just harassment. Where longstanding workers prevent new employees from doing certain tasks, a negative reputation will take hold. This applies to women as well as visible minorities (as in male employees regarding women hires as lacking in physical strength or skills to tackle something). If such issues are lurking in your workplace, you better fix them right away.

Tip #61 Search out successes and ask for details

Multiculturalism is no cakewalk, especially in the workplace. However, in today's Canada, a homogeneous workplace is no cakewalk either. There are plenty of success stories about organizations that have concentrated on being more inclusive and have prospered. Ask around and talk to those who have found their strategies successful. People are more than eager to talk about lessons they've learned.

Tip #62 Take failures with a grain of salt

It's easy to say, "The success stories about inclusive workforces must be true and the failures must be a lie," but when it comes to issues that challenge the status quo (i.e., seen as politically correct), take stories of failures with a grain of salt. In fact, whether you hear about a success or a failure, do your homework to make sure you're getting the straight goods. If someone says, "When Company X tried to hire women for those jobs, it was a disaster," feel free to call "Company X" and find out what really happened. I have run across a number of people who don't like their son being in competition with the sons and daughters of a wider applicant pool. Hence, they are more than happy to sabotage, talk negatively, or outright lie about programs that help to find the best candidates for a job. Changing the status quo has never been easy, but if you want your business to prosper in a changing society, then you need to change with it.

"It is better to understand little than to misunderstand a lot."

Anatole France

6

Management Needs To Know

David Wright was sitting at his desk two weeks after pulling what he considered a harmless Valentine's Day prank, when he was called to a meeting with two of the corporation's vice presidents. He was told that due to allegations of sexual harassment, he was to leave work and not return until a March 2nd meeting. Days later, at that meeting, he was given two choices: to resign or be fired. When he declined to resign, he was fired. This was 1992, and the organization for which Wright worked was the B.C. Trade Development Corporation in Vancouver.

What is it that led to Wright's firing? Two days before Valentine's Day, he and a colleague, Joe McKay, were discussing Valentine's Day celebrations over lunch, which somehow inspired McKay to buy some g-string panties on the way back to the office to send to fellow female employees as a joke. When McKay shared his idea with Wright, Wright hesitated, saying it sounded like a bad idea. But McKay insisted it would be taken as fun, and placed the g-strings in interoffice envelopes addressed to three women (including a vice president, Oksana Exell), penciling in the names of three male employees who were unaware of this prank, as the "gift" givers. He convinced Wright to mail the envelopes from his building, which Wright reluctantly did.

When Wright was called in that February day, he accepted responsibility for the mailing and suggested the company suspend him without pay, and order mandatory gender bias training, instead of holding to a resign-or-be-fired position. When the company rejected that idea and fired him, he took the company to court, claiming wrongful dismissal. The court accepted his version of the events and ruled that they did not justify his firing. Wright was awarded a year's salary plus expenses to the tune of approximately $90,000. After this defeat in court, the company decided to settle McKay's similar claim out of court.

This case received a lot of attention, especially in Vancouver. The provincial government of the day came under particular fire for the way the case was handled, because it owned the Trade Corporation. Public and government pundits also took issue with Exell, one of the women targeted, being promoted to president of the company prior to the decision being rendered. However, private or public, I think and the courts concur, that businesses have an obligation to take a strong stand on issues of human rights, including sexual harassment. By itself, the McKay and Wright "prank" easily falls into a perceived case of sexual intrusion, especially given that the senders did not identify themselves. (Worse, they tried to pass off the joke on innocent male employees.)

But Wright's case indicates that taking a strong stand can backfire, especially when held up against tough legal standards. Even a firm standing on principle takes its chances in court, never mind that the lawyers for Wright's employer must have advised the firm that it would probably win.

If nothing else, however, Wright, McKay and their employers all learned how to deal with incidents like this better in the future.

This chapter is about management's role and how important it is for managers and supervisors to understand human rights issues. Let's take a closer look at what the management of this company allowed in their

95

workplace around the time of the Wright case, as explored by the judge who handled the case.[19]

To enliven the office walls, employees pinned up a poster that in large block letters read, "Male Sex Object of the Month Award". Beneath this ran the statement, "This is to certify that William (Bill) Macho____ ...was Sex Object for the Month of November, 1989, at the Ministry of International Business and Immigration and the B.C. Trade Development Corporation". (Note: for the purposes of this book, I've left out Bill's last name) The poster had attracted many signatures of amused employees, including one from Oksana Exell, who wrote, "I can't believe I'm signing this! Oksana". Other signatures included "Luv ya Babe! You're the best!" and "Bill, where does the line-up start?"

Later that year, Bill was awarded a similar poster, which read, "This is to certify that Bill has, for the year 1990, attained the position (one of many he knows!!) of sex symbol of the year!!" And beneath that ran the line, "This award has never been held by any other individual, living or dead, for two consecutive years!"

Once again, the poster attracted many signatures on it, including the other two women who received the g-string panties. One of the women drew a heart after her name and wrote, "God created you. She did a great job. Love you." The other woman wrote, "To the sexiest man alive!" Clearly flattered by these two posters, Bill had both framed and hung on his office wall.

As if further evidence of an oversexed office is needed, please note that the company bulletin board was adorned with photos of rather scantily-dressed male dancers, in which the heads of the dancers had been replaced by photos of the heads of various men in the office.

Interesting scenario, right? Kind of puts a new light on things? It certainly makes me wonder what management was thinking, and what prompted them to go from there to taking a strong stand on harassment in Wright's case.

The moral of this story-and a significant point in this chapter-is that not all supervisors, managers or staff are up-to-date on human rights issues in the workplace, even though that can cost them big-time in the courts. Supervisors who participate in or look the other way regarding questionable behaviour aren't usually stupid; they just have plenty of other issues on their plate, and as we've seen many times in this book, the complexities of human rights issues need explaining. Of course, there are always some supervisors who don't agree with the law and therefore feel justified in flouting it.

The bottom line, however, is that senior management is responsible for ensuring that supervisors don't put the business at risk by violating human rights legislation.

From my perspective, most cases involve situations where management either misunderstood or did not care about their legal responsibilities. Here are some examples:

Human rights from a different angle

Managers usually think human rights cases only come from a human rights commission or tribunal. Hence, they tend to think their business is safe if they stay away from obvious human rights travesties like asking an employee for sex or telling an applicant that the company doesn't hire immigrants. But by now, readers of this book know that workplace human rights issues are not always obvious. For example, sexual harassment can involve negative attention applied to one predominant gender. Or policies that appear neutral but have a negative impact on certain groups, may be referred to as "adverse impact" or systemic discrimination. Hence, employers have to watch words and actions both in and around their workplace more closely than most think. And employers also have to watch *where* human rights issues may come from.

Years ago, I came across an Ontario Workers' Compensation Board (WCB)[20] appeals case involving a police officer in a Northern Ontario detachment, who made a claim of stress leave and was seeking compensation from the WCB. The case didn't look good for the officer, due to a number of factors. He had a drinking problem and fellow officers responded twice to calls from his home for domestic violence. During one, he threatened to commit suicide with his gun. As well, he was convicted under the Police Services Act for causing damage to his firearm and in another incident he wounded a friend in the wrist when his gun discharged while he was trying to repair it. There were other work-related issues that suggested the constable was not doing his job properly.

Although the WCB initially turned down his stress leave application, an appeals tribunal overturned that decision and granted him compensation. They reasoned that prior to all these incidents, the constable's wife had been sexually harassed by the officer's sergeant (the tribunal referred to it as "sexual misconduct"). When the constable and his wife, who also worked for the detachment, sought assistance for the sexual harassment issue, they were not supported at all. In fact, according to the tribunal, "The case was very poorly handled by the employer." One sergeant told the constable he should handle the issue "man to man" with his boss, while another warned about reporting on a superior when the officer was on probation. The appeals tribunal decided the constable's troublesome actions (the domestic disputes, gun use problems and work issues) all stemmed from the stress caused by the detachment's poor handling of the sexual harassment incidents.

Tip #63 Human rights aren't confined to a commission

This is but one of many examples across Canada where human rights matters appeared in proceedings other than a human rights commission or tribunal. Human rights issues can form part of probation, discipline or dismissal decisions. They can be an integral part of a labour arbitration, a court case on wrongful dismissal, an application for employment insurance or a WCB claim. Whenever they are raised, decision-makers often rule, or are expected to rule, on human rights procedures and law properly, or appeals will arise. And since human rights

> Because human rights legislation in Canada is given a preferred status, anyone deciding these issues must give them a lot of weight

legislation in Canada is given a preferred status, anyone deciding these issues must give them a lot of weight. In other words, when an employer's actions affect the human rights of employees and clients, these can be judged in many different venues, not just through a human rights commission.

From a business perspective, then, you need to be on the lookout for human rights issues that could be driving the problem. As with our police constable above, the police force was looking at his misconduct without looking at the root cause-the harassment of his wife and the detachment's abysmal way of dealing with it. If you get a whiff of a human rights element in a case, look into it closely. Better safe than broadsided.

Most issues are left alone

I've seen many reported cases of human rights violations occur due to supervisors and managers not doing the right thing. I found this to be the case in more than twenty-two years of working in the fields of human resources, labour/employee relations, and human rights. Why do some supervisors who are aware of a problem, fail to act on it or prevent further trouble? Here are my theories.

- *Not enough skills-*Ever since my first managerial job, I discovered we don't give supervisors enough support or training, especially when it comes to how to deal with people, conflict and human rights. Despite the plethora of courses on this topic today, many managers don't seem to have access to them. Instead, a select few seem to go to all of them.
- *Conflict adverse-*Most people don't want to deal with conflict. Superior species or not, when it comes to settling conflict, I think we're at the bottom of the food chain. You'll find me hanging out somewhere with the worms on this one because I hate conflict and prefer

99

everything being smooth. When someone is saying offensive things, or not accommodating a religious need, most people don't want to rock the boat. Even with training on conflict, it ain't easy to take on difficult issues.

• *Lack of support*-When a supervisor tries to do the right thing, he or she can often get blind-sided by a lack of support from the boss. My sister used to call up her "employment-specialist" brother for advice. We'd go over, in detail, a letter or a strategy to deal with a problem employee, but when all was said and done, I'd have to ask why she bothered. She knew her boss would cave in, and nothing would get done. Supervisors at a higher level are just as conflict adverse as the rest of us.

• *Office politics*-Who's related to whom or whose friends are associated with whom are factors that often get in the way of dealing with human rights issues. Reported human rights cases are stuffed full of examples of an employee not bringing an issue to a supervisor, manager or owner because the problem employee is close to the boss. If, as a result, the boss had no idea what was happening, does that excuse him or her? Nope. Lots of tribunals will conclude that the boss should have known what was going on in the workplace, that he or she was willfully blind.

Tip #64 Simple actions will pay off

If your business or organization takes on the obvious human rights issues that come to the attention of a supervisor or manager, you will be far, far ahead of most workplaces. And you'll be surprised how easily many of the problems can be resolved. A simple comment like "Knock it off" when someone makes a sexist joke, or an effort to chat with a colleague about the potential liability in refusing to hire a certain employee, can go a long way to resolving real or potential problems. The law books are full or cases where people didn't take on the simplest of problems when they arose.

When it's not on your radar screen

Leaving something alone because you either don't want to deal with it or you aren't sure how to deal with it, is very different from not thinking about it. There are plenty of times when insensitive statements or injustices take place and they don't even turn up on our radar screens because we're not tuned into things that can be a problem for another person.

Years ago I was co-facilitating a diversity training session with a colleague. The contract was mine and I was able to select my co-facilitators. Being a white guy myself, I wanted to reflect diversity as much as possible, so I got a woman to co-facilitate half of the sessions and brought on an Aboriginal colleague for the other half. During a break at one of the sessions, my co-facilitator Liz turned to me and asked, "What are we going to do about that comment?" When I asked, "What comment?", I was surprised to hear her repeat a comment both of us had heard, but which hadn't registered for me. I can't remember the exact comment, but it was derogatory towards women, and the minute Liz brought it up, I was surprised I had let it pass without saying anything. It was as useful a lesson to me as it was to participants. Clearly I hadn't felt the sting Liz had. I realized that being a man, I don't feel the sting a woman feels, because I'm not in her shoes. I can feel for a woman. I can understand why she feels badly. I can even flinch when a sexist comment was made. But I don't feel the sting a woman feels.

> Unless you're part of the group affected, you rarely feel the sting of a hurtful comment.

Regardless of who feels what sting, the important thing is to be supportive when we know others are affected by hurtful language. When I do catch such a comment, I'm not interested in shaming anybody. I'm interested in talking about the comment and dealing with its ramifications. Above all, I want to make sure participants don't think I agree with the comment by my silence.

Tip #65 Create an environment where people speak up

If a workplace environment is such that people feel comfortable bringing up and dealing with issues, a simple explanation is often all you'll need. Some situations, however, will call for a greater deal of explanation and understanding. For example, referring to "native time" might seem harmless or even light when one is referring to an Aboriginal co-worker being late, but to your Aboriginal colleague, it can be offensive, because it buys into the stereotype that they are lazy.

Complexity of human rights

In 1999, the Supreme Court of Canada brought down what I consider to be the most significant human rights decision to date: the decision discussed in chapter 2 that allowed Tawney Meiorin to get her job back (she was the fire fighter let go for not passing stringent physical fitness tests). When the court ruled that Meiorin's employer had to accommodate her, it essentially threw out the difference between direct and adverse impact discrimination when it came to accommodation. Confused? You're not alone. I was always struggling with the formula the court previously offered for interpreting discrimination and accommodation.

My point is this: If justices on the Supreme Court had to change their direction on an important principle of Canadian human rights to make it more understandable, then perhaps the rest of us can cut ourselves some slack for grappling with these issues. Of course, the reality is, the Supreme Court of Canada can change its mind, move in a different direction or set new laws, but the rest

> If the top legal minds of Canada struggle with human rights issues, we need to cut ourselves some slack

of us won't know the result until *after* its decision is made. By that time, we may have followed one of their other paths, or thought we understood where the law stood on an issue.

So, frontline supervisors and managers at all levels must ensure that their basic day-to-day dealings don't offend the important, liberal and ever-changing principles of human rights. When one employee makes inappropriate sexual comments to a colleague: Piece of cake. Easy one. When an employee, weeks in advance, asks for a vacation day to celebrate a significant religious day, another easy one. But what if during a typical lunch break at which employees are sharing tales of their dating successes and failures, a gay employee starts talking about his romantic life, and a straight, religious employee objects? How do you deal with these competing rights? What if a female employee flirts with all her male colleagues but one? In fact, what if he tries to join in and she accuses him of sexual harassment? What do you do with those?

The laws spell out answers, but without easy access to legal journals or the company lawyer, most supervisors wouldn't know. The problem is not a lack of legislation, but a lack of discussion of human rights issues, or a lack of discussions that go beyond simple textbook cases. Most people are intimidated by the complexities and legalities, and this leads them to refuse to do anything, or to make very arbitrary decisions that don't take rights into consideration.

Tip #66 Give supervisors and managers the basics

By all means, consult company lawyers or other human resources specialists when you feel it's important to do so. But go the next step, too: Endeavour to train all levels of supervisors and managers on the basics, then challenge them to think about common-sense ways to deal with less traditional problems that arise.

Being off-side

"You can't legislate (take your pick) decency/politeness/civility/morality." Have you ever heard that before? Over the years, I've certainly heard it in the context of human rights, but I don't agree with it. I think human rights legislation has changed the way people behave, and that in turn has begun changing some of the ways we think, even our values. Legislation years ago outlawed racial slurs in the workplace. Now most people flinch when they hear someone making a racist comment. Years ago, cab companies used to put up with

> Legislating human rights has changed the way we behave and think, even our values

customers' racist requests for not sending cabbies of a certain ethnic background. Then they were stung by civil liberties and human rights groups who exposed them for doing so. Today you'd be hard-pressed to find a cab company in Canada submitting to such requests. Some companies will ignore them for fear of being caught, and others because the dispatcher knows it's not right.

Tip #67 Get your workforce on-side, at least at work

We've come a long way on certain issues, but human rights involve relatively liberal thinking and an openness to accept differences. Many aren't accepting of that, and therefore aren't on-side with issues involving human rights. Your workplace likely reflects the full spectrum of thoughts and values on human rights, even among managers. By law, however, and by Canadian standards, you must get them on-side.

A policy is not enough

In the spring of 1997, the media was full of stories about British Columbia's Simon Fraser University and its firing of swim coach Liam Donnelly amidst allegations of sexual harassment made by student Rachel Marsden. Yet after all was said and done, Liam Donnelly was rehired, Rachel Marsden was given $12,000 as a settlement for counseling and other expenses, John Stubbs was no longer the university's president (although he was given a severance of almost $300,000), the university paid Donnelly's $60,000 legal bill, and the university conducted a formal review of previous harassment and discrimination cases. Throughout this period, the university felt the impact on its fundraising. A *Globe and Mail* headline noted, "SFU's

Costs in Sex Case Exceed $350,000," but when I do the math and consider all the time and resources involved in cleaning up this mess, I reckon that figure is extremely conservative.

The university also went to great expense to create a new policy and procedure for dealing with future harassment investigations. According to the university's 1998 annual report, this is a simplified explanation of the new procedure at SFU's Harassment Resolution Office:

Under the revised policy, formal harassment allegations are referred to a board chair, who can authorize or refuse to authorize an investigation. The seven-person board provides advice to a vice president. If an investigation is required, the board chair appoints an experienced investigator with expertise in administrative law, who may order a comprehensive fact-finding search, at which point the report goes to the chair, who forwards it to a senior university official-and so on and so on.

What do you think of that? Can you visualize the fast-inflating bills? After the dust settled at SFU, I looked into their previous policy and procedures, compared them with the new process, and concluded that SFU used to have a really great automatic Buick...but drove it like an old rented standard Volkswagen Beetle with John Belushi's character from Animal House at the wheel. Now I think they have a top-of-the-line Jaguar with a full-time chauffeur.

Tip #68 Apply policies properly and with common sense

You don't need a top-of-the-line anything. Many workplaces have a policy covering sexual and other forms of harassment. Some policies cover other human rights issues. I don't really care if there is a policy or not (okay, I'll admit it is easier if there is one), as long as the workplace adheres to the law and common decency. Keep in mind that not only did SFU have a policy; it had paid staff dedicated solely to handling harassment complaints. Yet look at the trouble the institution got into! Most workplaces don't have those kinds of resources and most don't need it if supervisors and employees understand the *importance* of a harassment-free workplace-*and* act on it with common sense. SFU is living proof that having a policy doesn't always save an organization, especially where it is not applied properly.

When it comes to human rights, the supervisors' role is to ensure a good, basic understanding of human rights procedures and a focused application of these. Mistakes will happen and some decisions will be reversed, but if staff are taught the basics and told to ask for advice when unsure, most workplaces will run more smoothly.

Liability

When supervisors do not enforce policies according to the law, the organization or individuals within it may be legally liable. In Canada, the award of general damages isn't very large (not to sneeze at $2,000 to $10,000) but other costs tend to escalate: legal fees, payment of costs for the opposing side, out-of-pocket expenses, and lost wages if applicable. Meanwhile, the time required to deal with a formal case costs a lot in lost productivity, stress and anxiety-all of which coexist with your need to carry on business as usual, since your work doesn't stop for a legal proceeding.

More and more, employers will be held liable for what happens in their workplace. In the eyes of the law, either they knew what was going on or they should have known what was going on, and in both cases, that means they take responsibility and pay the awards. Personal liability seems to flow to those actively involved in the process. In other words, if a supervisor was involved in discrimination or in covering it up when he or she found out about the discrimination, that's the person most likely to be found personally liable. The complainant may go after that supervisor, not just the corporation or department, for the award.

> Personal liability generally occurs only when management is actively involved in the process

In 1992, the Supreme Court of Canada formally brought unions into the human rights legal liability equation with a decision involving an employer and union judged to have not sufficiently accommodated a religious employee's scheduling needs. It probably came as a surprise to members of the Canadian Union of Public Employees (CUPE) to find their union dues going to a hefty legal bill, since CUPE has been at the forefront of human rights issues for decades. However, the notion that all parties in the employment equation may find themselves liable if they don't actively take part in resolving human rights issues was an important lesson to learn.

> Given that their union had been involved in human rights issues for decades, CUPE members were undoubtedly surprised when the Supreme Court indicated they were liable

Tip #69 Threats of liability should create incentives

Because money, or the threat of losing it, is so important in our society, the issue of liability is a good reason to ensure supervisors and managers know as much as possible regarding human rights.

Parting Tips for Management Needs To Know

Tip #70 Discuss human rights issues regularly

Supervisors and managers don't need a law degree to understand the basics of human rights for the workplace and client services. However, on a regular basis, cover issues of human rights in the same way you would for health and safety issues, profit projections or cost containments. All of these will be affected if a human rights issue becomes formal in your workplace.

Tip #71 Encourage real dialogue on human rights issues

Discussions about human rights don't have to be lectures. I find the best approach is to allow colleagues to bring up real examples and discuss them. It moves a talk from the clinical to the real. For example, if you have a female supervisor in a group of otherwise male supervisors, get her to tell the men why certain words or actions are a problem. If your workplace is in anyway caring, such discussions will go much further than stern prohibitions of, say, sexist language. Such dialogues must, I repeat *must*, be done in a non-judgmental format where people aren't blamed. If discussions raise an "I didn't know that" response, you've got the right mix.

Tip #72 Allow for different thoughts

Human rights decisions sometimes fly in the face of what we think of as equality. Supervisors and managers might not understand why they need to give a person with a disability certain concessions at work in order to meet legal requirements of accommodation. Allow supervisors to be frustrated with concepts and results, as long as it leads to understanding. They don't have to agree with it, but they have to adhere to it. If your management team knows that the thought police aren't going to arrest their minds, they'll feel better about having to change only their behaviours, not their minds.

Tip #73 Stress consistency

Make sure supervisors and managers know they must be consistent in order to be firm about human rights violations. This chapter kicked off with a strong example of inconsistency: the B.C. Trade Development Corporation allowing "sex object of the month awards" at the same time as it was handing out tough discipline regarding sexual harassment. When a dilemma arises, encourage your supervisors to think, "What if I allowed this to happen with a different group?" For example, don't allow an employee to constantly degrade Christians when you know you'd take a strong stand on similar degradation against Muslims or Jews.

Tip #74 Encourage supervisors to admit mistakes

When a supervisor has made a big mistake-perhaps allowed a horrible racist joke to be told without responding

-encourage him or her to admit and correct the error. It could be as easy as offering an apology. Victims of workplace human rights violations usually want a reasonable remedy, not money. Human rights law is by definition "remedial" legislation, so it's a lot easier to correct a mistake than people think. Human rights cases typically start because someone in management didn't get involved when they should have. Allow for all levels of supervisors to admit mistakes to their bosses and their employees, without fear.

> "The world is full of people whose notion of a satisfactory future is, in fact, a return to the idealized past."
>
> Robertson Davies

7

Changing With The Times

In the 1970s and 1980s, *John Turner* was Canada's prime minister in waiting, basking in almost Kennedy-like status in Canada. Yet in 1984, after being lured to take over the Liberal leadership and therefore the prime minister's post, he and his party went down in one of its worst defeats, losing to Brian Mulroney and the Progressive Conservatives. Why did he suffer such a hard landing?

One reason that still stands out in my mind is the fact that he got caught "patting" Iona Campagnolo's bottom. Having worked her way up from local politics, Campagnolo had been a federal Cabinet minister, a recipient of the Order of Canada, and at the time of the patting, was the first woman president of the Liberal Party of Canada. Canadian women were furious.

This wasn't the first time the prime minister had been caught patting the bottoms of prominent women-or women in general. But until that year, the media hadn't made an issue of it. However, when Campagnolo patted Turner in return, in front of television cameras during the election campaign, it became a campaign issue. Instead of apologizing right away, Turner tried to minimize the incident. Political cartoonists, editorial writers, and international newspapers promptly had a field day.

"It would be twenty-three days before Turner would apologize for his gesture-twenty-four days in which the word 'bum' became part of everyday Canadian vocabulary, always with Turner's hand attached," Charles Lynch wrote in his book *Race for the Rose*.

When asked to explain his actions, Turner said, "It's tangible, it's tactile, it's face to face, mano a mano." Funny how his tactile nature didn't have him patting men's bums.

How did this happen? Why would a man, knowing cameras are on his every move during a national election, not stay clear of something that in 1984 every woman and virtually every man in the country knew was wrong? How did this get past his political advisors?

I think the truth is that Turner lived in a world of prominence, power and influence, and no one challenged him on habits that for many men would have ended up with a slap in the face. The goalposts moved, and no one bothered to tell him. In the past, the John Turners of the world have gotten away with incidents that would put the rest of us out of jobs, or have us facing substantial consequences.

The lesson here is that even if prominent people continue to enjoy breaks or second chances, in the end, tolerance of inappropriate behaviour is fast disappearing.

This chapter is designed to look at the low tolerance for inappropriate words and actions regarding basic human rights. I use examples of prominent people, not to try to sell this chapter to *Vanity Fair*, but to put everyone on notice that individuals at all levels of business had better be respectful of people's basic human rights or face harsh consequences. In each example, we'll see where and why something went wrong.

> Individuals at all levels of a business had better be respectful of people's basic human rights, or face harsh consequences

This chapter consists of two parts. The first part deals with people like John Turner, who failed to keep up with the times, and the folks around them who do them a disservice by allowing them to continue. The second deals with people who, in some small way, tried to "fit in" with a group, and ended up with regrettable professional consequences.

Not keeping up with the times

David Ahenakew served in Canada's army, reaching the rank of sergeant and receiving the Canadian Decoration for distinguished service and good conduct. In 1967, he joined the Federation of Saskatchewan Indian Nations (FSIN) and a year later became its chief for a decade, eventually securing a record as the longest serving chief. In 1978, Ahenakew became a recipient of the Order of Canada. The University of Regina gave him an Honourary Doctorate of Laws for his involvement in establishing the Saskatchewan Indian Federated College at the University. To top it all off, he became the national grand chief of the Assembly of First Nations from 1982 until 1985. During his term as grand chief, Ahenakew spoke to a parliamentary inquiry, chastising Canadians for harboring racist views.

Given his distinguished past, many people were surprised at the content of a speech Ahenakew delivered to almost two hundred delegates attending a Federation of Saskatchewan Indian Nations conference on Aboriginal health care in 2002. During a forty-five minute address filled with profanities, Ahenakew referred to immigrants as "god-damned immigrants," complained about bigotry, and blamed the media for racial conflict. He talked about his time in Europe with the Canadian military, where Germans told him that Jews had started the Second World War and how they, along with the Americans, were going to start a third world war.

"My great-grandson goes to school in Saskatoon," he said during his speech. "These god-damned immigrants - East Indians, Pakistanis, Afghanistans, whites and so forth-call him a dirty little Indian. He's the cleanest of the god-damn works there."[21]

After the speech, a reporter asked Ahenakew to explain his comments. According to the *CBC*, he replied, "The Jews damn-near owned all of Germany prior to the war. That's how Hitler came in, and he was going to make damn sure that the Jews didn't take over Germany or Europe. That's why he fried six million of those guys, you know. How do you get rid of a, you know, a disease like that, that's going to take over, that's going to dominate, that's going to everything? To hell with the Jews. I can't stand them and that's it."[22]

Condemnation was swift from most Canadian leaders, Aboriginal and non-Aboriginal. Ahenakew ended up resigning from all Aboriginal leadership positions, and was criminally charged with willfully promoting hatred against an identifiable group. As this book was going to press, the advisory council for the Order of Canada was awaiting the outcome of the criminal charges before deciding if his membership should be revoked. (To date, Alan Eagleson is the only recipient who has been stripped of his membership, and that was for being convicted of fraud.)

There are two aspects to this story that are as disturbing as the words Ahenakew used that day. First, he had repeatedly made racist comments in the past about Jews, African Americans and East Indians without repercussions. In an article for the *Saskatoon Star Phoenix*, columnist Doug Cuthand-a man with family and past work connections to Ahenakew-wrote, "He just kind of lumped them together as foreign-born bastards." [23]

Cuthand told *CBC TV National* reporter Jo Lynn Sheane, "I was surprised he said it to a reporter, but I wasn't surprised he would say [such words] because he'd said them in private before. He has his dark side, and he was protected by people in the organization to-you know-keep that dark side under wraps. This time it just came out." [24]

This leads to the second disturbing point-the lack of concern for Ahenakew's comments by delegates and leaders at the December conference. While many of the offensive comments were made to reporter James Parker of the *Saskatoon Star Phoenix*, there was enough offense in his comments made at the podium. None of the delegates spoke up to condemn Ahenakew's comments, and others were downright angry that the story was reported. Given that the media had been invited to cover health-care changes affecting Aboriginals, it's easy to understand that the FSIN didn't want this story hijacking their conference. However, Ahenakew was not just a speaker; he was an awarded elder, a former FSIN chief and an FSIN senator-a role model. Did they really expect the media to treat him like a guy off the street, someone from whom the organization could distance themselves?

And yet FSIN Vice Chief Lawrence Joseph, who sat at the conference table where Ahenakew made his initial comments, accused the media of "selling newspapers on the backs of Indians". He told a *Star Phoenix* reporter, "It's f-ing garbage. What was your intent to print that story? Why would you do that? It's just one person's opinion. I'm too angry about this reckless attack by the press."

FSIN chief Perry Bellegarde, who hadn't attended the conference, said afterwards, "It's not an official position of anybody except Dave Ahenakew. That's where it rests. He's entitled to his opinion. We, as indigenous peoples, are fighting for our survival. We also push peaceful co-existence between our peoples and everybody else."[25]

Both of these men were roundly criticized by FSIN members and leaders-as well as the general population-for not taking a forceful stand against the comments by Ahenakew. They had to backtrack as the story received top billing across Canada and their leader was widely condemned by other Canadian leaders.

Why didn't any of the delegates or conference leaders condemn Ahenakew's outrageous comments outright? Why had they let him get away with racist comments in the past? Even if the comments were made in private, colleagues owed it to him, because he was a leader in his community, to raise objections. I wonder if anyone, at some point, had told him he would some day get in trouble for spouting his views?

Ahenakew's formerly distinguished career is now in tatters; he has lost his ability to help Aboriginals at so many levels. And Aboriginal communities across Canada are spending valuable time and money healing the wounds he inflicted.

> Because of his racist comments, Ahenakew's formerly distinguished career is now in tatters

Unfortunately, the Federation of Saskatchewan Indian Nations' leadership did not understand the gravity of Ahenakew's comments, or how it affected their association. On January 27, 2004, with banner headlines in the *National Post*, it was revealed that the FSIN put Ahenakew's name forward to the national Assembly of First Nations to sit on a federally funded aboriginal commission. After an outcry from Jewish organizations across Canada, two days later the Assembly of First Nations stated Ahenakew would not be sitting on the new commission.

Tip #75 Encourage strong and courageous stands

It's tough to stand up to someone who holds a prominent position in the community. Suddenly you find "little ol' me" against a person with an impressive resume. It's even more challenging in the workplace, where you rely on your job to make a living. You may feel like David up against Goliath.

So what do you do when someone makes racist, sexist or homophobic comments? What do you do when it's from a distinguished person? What do you do when you're caught off guard?

• First, don't worry about being caught off guard. If words don't come to you immediately, collect your thoughts and find a way to say them later. If, however, someone else speaks up on the spot, support that person. You know what it took for him or her to say something.

- Don't be afraid to return to the issue; it's never too late, even if what you wanted to say at the time comes to you in the middle of a meeting or a workplace gathering. If it's weighing on your mind, it's likely weighing on the minds of others.

- Stick to the issue, and if the perpetrator wants to sidetrack by pointing out the bad habits of others, insist on sticking to the words that caused you to speak up.

- Whatever you do, don't try to soft-pedal a situation when strong words are warranted. No need to lambaste a person who made an outrageous comment, but it's really important that the person know your workplace won't tolerate such comments.

- Be prepared to stand alone. Because most employees are conflict averse, you may find others unwilling to join you. You'll have to decide if it's worth it for you.

Most of the time, you as a supervisor won't be faced with comments like Ahenakew's. Thank goodness. But when you hear inappropriate comments, find a way to say something. Precisely because he had rarely been challenged in private, Ahenakew thought he could get away with his comments in public. But public or private, people need to know there's no audience for words that go against basic human rights.

> Public or private, people need to know there's no audience for words that go against basic human rights

Thomas Haythe was a Harvard graduate and prominent lawyer with the New York firm Haythe and Curley, which in October of 1999 announced a merger with top Toronto law firm Tory Tory DesLauriers & Binnington. The new firm, named Tory Haythe, would employ three hundred lawyers in Toronto and New York serving an impressive list of business clients.

Just six weeks after the merger announcement, the firm's New York lawyers, including Haythe, attended dinner parties at the homes of senior partners in Toronto as a way of getting to know one another. The celebrations carried on with drinks and dancing downtown. We'll never know exactly what Haythe got up to during the partying, but we know it involved alcohol and a number of female colleagues, and was severe enough that managing partner Les Viner declared the incidents to be violations of the firm's harassment policy.

After front-page attention in the *Globe and Mail* and *National Post* newspapers, Haythe, sixty years old at the time, went on medical leave and indicated he would not be returning to the firm. Haythe revealed to Viner that he was being tested for a brain tumour. The newly merged firm promptly reduced its name to Torys LLP, eliminating reference to the New Yorker who used to head his own firm.

The incident was dealt with swiftly in hopes of avoiding extensive negative public relations and legal consequences. In years past, a man of Haythe's stature would almost certainly have had enough clout to prevent the firm from taking meaningful action. But today is a different story. This newly merged firm would have been ridiculed for allowing sexual harassment to go unchecked inside its walls while giving advice to businesses about avoiding similar problems. Even had they been able to weather the bad press, they'd certainly have lost business. Some businesswomen would surely have taken their business elsewhere, or demanded a change of law firms from their own employers.

Tip #76 Deal with harassment even from the "top"

When the Haythe rumours first broke, they ran like wildfire through the legal community. I'm sure people reading the story must have thought it a bizarre irony that this could happen not only to a law firm-never mind one of Canada's most prominent-but to one of the most senior partners of the newly merged firm. Though we're no longer surprised to hear about sexual harassment in general, we don't expect it to happen in big-time law firms.

117

We've got to get past that and realize that sexual harassment, inappropriate comments, inappropriate behaviours and sexual stereotyping can happen at any and all Canadian workplaces. Take for example, one the highest legal benches in Canada.

Alberta Court of Appeal Justice *John McClung* received a letter of reprimand on May 19, 1999 from three of Canada's top judges, for a letter he wrote and a subsequent interview he gave to the *National Post*. These three members of the Canadian Judicial Council, a body with a mandate to handle complaints against federally appointed judges, were responding to twenty-four formal complaints against McClung.

It all started when McClung wrote a decision regarding a sexual assault case involving a seventeen-year-old woman (the complainant) and Steve Ewanchuk, a man almost three times her age and close to twice her size. In hopes of getting a job with Ewanchuk's woodworking business, the complainant met with him at his van and trailer in the parking lot of an Edmonton mall. The two spent more than two hours in the van, then trailer. During that time, Ewanchuk touched the complainant inappropriately several times, laid down on top of her, ground his pelvis into hers, took out his penis and placed it on her leg, then paid her $100, asking her not to say anything. At each stage, the complainant said "no" or made it clear she was not comfortable with the situation. After the interview was over, the complainant contacted the police and criminal charges of sexual assault were brought against Ewanchuk. He was acquitted of sexual assault at a trial. When the Crown appealed Ewanchuk's acquittal to the Alberta Court of Appeal, Judges McClung and Foisy upheld the acquittal although Alberta Chief Justice Fraser dissented saying Ewanchuk should have been found guilty.

In his decision, McClung noted that while the complainant was scared, she showed no signs of her fear to Ewanchuk, in hopes that he would not turn violent. On this basis, McClung felt she did not give Ewanchuk the proper signs of withholding consent. He read his Chief

Justice's dissenting decision before writing his own, then made the comments that started his problems: "The Chief Justice's concerns aside, it must be pointed out that the complainant did not present herself to Ewanchuk or enter his trailer in a bonnet and crinolines. She told Ewanchuk that she was the mother of a six-month-old baby and that, along with her boyfriend, she shared an apartment with another couple. (I must point out these aspects of the trial record, but with no intention of denigrating her or lessening the legal protection to which she was entitled.)"[26]

McClung also referred to Ewanchuk indicating "romantic intentions" and making "clumsy passes" toward the complainant. In the last paragraph of his decision, McClung added, "In my reading of the trial record, this Crown appeal must be dismissed. Beyond the error of law issue, the sum of the evidence indicates that Ewanchuk's advances to the complainant were far less criminal than hormonal. In a less litigious age, going too far in the boyfriend's car was better dealt with on site-a well-chosen expletive, a slap in the face or, if necessary, a well-directed knee." [27]

When the case was appealed to the Supreme Court of Canada, the judges unanimously agreed to overturn the decision and convict Ewanchuk for sexual assault. While she agreed with the rest of her colleagues, Justice Claire L'Heureux-Dubé (with Justice Charles Gonthier concurring) decided to add some comments of her own. In strongly worded reasoning, she responded to all of McClung's comments noted above:

> *Even though McClung J.A. asserted that he had no intention of denigrating the complainant, one might wonder why he felt necessary to point out these aspects of the trial record. Could it be to express that the complainant is not a virgin? Or that she is a person of questionable moral character because she is not married and lives with her boyfriend and another couple? These comments made by an appellate judge help reinforce the myth that under such circumstances, either the*

119

*complainant is less worthy of belief, she invited the sex-
ual assault, or her sexual experience signals probable
consent to further sexual activity. Based on those attrib-
uted assumptions, the implication is that if the complainant articulates her lack of consent by saying "no,"
she really does not mean it, and even if she does, her
refusal cannot be taken as seriously as if she were a girl
of "good" moral character.* [28]

Finally, L'Heureux-Dubé directed her statements to
Alberta judges McClung and Foisy and got to the heart of
this issue-myths, stereotypes and bias:

*Complainants should be able to rely on a system free
from myths and stereotypes, and on a judiciary whose
impartiality is not compromised by these biased
assumptions. The [Criminal] Code was amended in 1983
and in 1992 to eradicate reliance on those assumptions;
they should not be permitted to resurface through the
stereotypes reflected in the reasons of the majority of the
Court of Appeal. It is part of the role of this Court to
denounce this kind of language, unfortunately still used
today, which not only perpetuates archaic myths and
stereotypes about the nature of sexual assaults, but also
ignores the law.* [29]

This stern language from Canada's top bench to
Alberta's top bench inspired headlines across the country.
The next day, February 26, 1999, a two-paragraph letter to
the editor appeared in the *National Post* as follows:

*Madam Justice Claire L'Heureux-Dube's graceless slide
into personal invective in Thursday's judgment in the
Ewanchuk case allows some response. It issued with
"the added bitterness of an old friend."*
*Whether the Ewanchuk case will promote the fundamen-
tal right of every accused Canadian to a fair trial will
have to be left to the academics. Yet there may be one
immediate benefit. The personal convictions of the
judge, delivered again from her judicial chair, could*

provide a plausible explanation for the disparate (and growing) number of male suicides being reported in the Province of Quebec.
Mr. Justice J. W. McClung, Court of Appeal of Alberta, Edmonton. [30]

Once again, a flood of media attention focused on the Alberta judge. The following day, the *National Post* ran a front-page story about reporter Shawn Ohler's conversation with McClung. In that article, the judge was quoted as saying the complainant "was not lost on her way home from the nunnery" and she had been "portrayed as a wide-eyed little girl who didn't know what was happening to her. Well, come on, now."

McClung's letter's reference to the growing number of male suicides in Quebec really caught people's attention, as L'Heureux-Dubé's husband had committed suicide more than twenty years earlier. McClung said he had not known this.

What's the lesson here? Even at what is supposed to be the highest and most intelligent workplaces in the country, we can still hear disturbing comments and outdated stereotypes. It's certainly bad enough that in 1998, the two judges on the Alberta Court of Appeal were willing to refer to Ewanchuk's actions as "hormonal" and "romantic". It's also very unfortunate that McClung not only held onto his notion that the complainant was somewhat responsible for what took place, but shared that with the a national newspaper.

But the big issue to consider is that McClung launched arguably personal attacks against L'Heureux-Dubé, yet not on any of the male Supreme Court judges (who, like L'Heureux-Dubé, had disagreed with McClung's acquittal). Nor did he comment on Mr. Justice Gonthier's concurrence with what L'Heureux-Dubé wrote.

This, combined with the male suicide comments, prompted the Canadian Judicial Council panel of Nova Scotia Chief Justice Constance Glube, Quebec Chief Justice Pierre Michaud and Ontario Chief Justice Roy McMurtry to express strong disapproval. They looked into the actions of McClung regarding his letter to the editor and his follow-up media interview. They also looked at his comments in the Ewanchuk case and another case involving Delwin Vriend, who was fired from his job at an Alberta college for being gay. Justice McClung and Justice O'Leary decided in 1996 that Mr. Vriend's rights were not violated, but the Supreme Court of Canada overturned that decision and said Alberta had to include "sexual orientation" protection in their human rights legislation.

Because McClung apologized, and due to his long and distinguished career as a lawyer and judge, the panel decided not to formally investigate his actions further and therefore he held onto his job.

However, the seven-page letter they issued is filled with comments such as "inappropriate conduct," "entirely inappropriate," "not valid claims," "not credible," "significant indiscretion" and "simply unacceptable". Regarding parts of his decision in the Vriend case, they said, "The Panel has concluded that your comments cross beyond the boundary of even the wide latitude given to judges in expressing their reasons. They have no logical connection to the issues in the case and detract from respect for equality rights. They constitute inappropriate conduct for a judge." [31]

Finally, the judges wrote, "In sum, the Panel has found your conduct to be inappropriate but not malicious or reflecting oblique motive. The Panel expects that you will learn from this experience in dealing with future cases."

Tip #77 There can be consequences at the highest levels

When I talk about this case, some people-especially women-are outraged that McClung got away with what seems like a slap on the wrist. You may feel, like many do, that McClung should have been removed from the bench for his sexist and homophobic language and beliefs. While the panel didn't see it that way, it certainly put the Alberta judge on notice that not only will his inflammatory language be censured, but his decisions will be overturned if he is not keeping up with the times in Canada. In the world of senior judges, those are serious consequences.

The irony on this issue comes from McClung's heritage. Many will recognize the name, since McClung is the grandson of famed Canadian suffragette Nellie McClung. In October 2000, McClung and four other famous Canadian women were honoured with a monument on Parliament Hill, the first time the National Capital Commission allowed a statue that didn't include monarchs, dead prime ministers or Fathers of Confederation on Parliament Hill. These "Famous Five" women won the case at the Privy Council of the House of Lords in London in 1929, ensuring that Canadian women were "persons" when it came to appointments to the Senate under the British North America Act.

Is this case just an exercise in modern day feminism? Do we worry only about high ranking and highly paid judges doing verbal battle? Madame Justice L'Heureux-Dubé felt strongly about this case because of prevalent harm to women. It seems she was right about this case, and this criminal, because on July 24, 2003, when Steve Ewanchuk was released from prison, the Edmonton Police department issued a warning. Although he had served his sentence for the case noted above, the police indicated that he remains a "high-risk sexual offender and poses a risk of significant harm to the community".

Both the Haythe and McClung incidents make it clear that times have changed. Though many are still getting away with bad behaviour, loads of examples prove that employees now realize they have basic legal rights allowing them to complain, and they are asserting these. True, sometimes a workplace policy or law isn't enough to encourage people to speak up, but that's all the more reason to make sure your workplace is one in which people do feel comfortable speaking up. Hearing a complaint may cause you pain; you may wish the problem had never arisen in the first place, but to be an employer of choice, you want to hear about these problems so you can deal with them.

The second part of this chapter deals with the need we all feel to fit in and how that can get us into trouble, especially when human rights are thrown into the equation.

Fitting in

Detective *Scott Driemel* served as both spokesperson for the Vancouver Police Department and a spokesperson for the joint Vancouver Police-RCMP missing women's task force. (The latter was assembled to investigate the whereabouts and subsequently the murders of women, many of who were prostitutes and street people, who disappeared from Vancouver's Downtown East Side.)

At a conference of senior police officers in June of 2002, Driemel made jokes later described as insensitive and sexist towards women. One of the punch lines made references to women's body parts, while another made a play on the word "hooker". The Vancouver Police Officers Association, which represents senior officers, made a complaint to the police chief at the time, Terry Blythe. In response, Driemel volunteered to write ninety-three letters of apology to participants at the conference. Once the families of the missing and dead women heard about this, and it reached the media in November 2002, they wanted him removed from this sensitive and important job. They got their wish.

Although the new police chief, Jamie Graham, insisted that the incident was behind them and Driemel would stay in his job, two days later he announced the acceptance of Driemel's request for reassignment out of the position of media spokesperson for both the Vancouver Police and the joint task force. A couple of jokes cost Mr. Driemel a very prominent and sought-after job.

Why, on such a sensitive topic as women, would Driemel make these jokes to a crowd of people? I think we get clues from some of the statements he made to the press. *The Vancouver Sun* quoted Driemel as saying, "I thought I was dealing with a bunch of crusty police people, but in retrospect, I should have recognized that nowadays when you are speaking to any public group, you've got to err on the side of absolute correctness." [32]

It's easy to make mistakes trying to "fit in". It doesn't mean we're insecure; it just means we want to please a certain group. We let them know that we're "one of the guys" by saying things we think they'll want to hear. I've done it many times.

Driemel's desire to fit in with "a bunch of crusty police people" prompted him to say something he thought they'd get a kick out of. I don't think for a moment he wanted to degrade women. Yet like so many of us, he hadn't clued into the fact that the rules have changed. Even crusty old men have wives, daughters and granddaughters who give them an earful when they get out of line on issues of gender equality, sometimes even helping them "get it" in the process. Once they've got it, they're not just paying lip service when women family members are present. They actually speak up at work.

> Many of us are slow to recognize when the rules change

Tip #78 Beware of trying to "fit in" with others

Reflect on the number of times in familiar surroundings you do something-perhaps deviating slightly from your norm-meant to help you fit in with a certain group of people. Now reflect on the up-side versus the down-side, and you may avoid the hard lesson that Driemel learned.

At a higher level of a different organizational echelon, here's an incident that took place with similar career repercussions.

Trent Lott had it all. After the mid-term elections of November 2002, he was the Republican's Senate Majority Leader at a time when the United States Republican Party had control of the White House, the House of Representatives and the Senate. However, that all changed with one birthday party.

On December 6, 2002, Senator Lott was helping the president and other dignitaries celebrate the 100th birthday of then-Senator Strom Thurmond from South Carolina (he retired in January 2003 and died June 26, 2003). In 1948, Thurmond had run for the presidency of the United States on a pro-segregationist ticket-promising to keep Blacks and Whites separate and unequal.

At this birthday party, Lott noted publicly that back in 1948, his state, Mississippi, had voted for Thurmond and his segregationist platform. Lott said, "We're proud of it, and if the rest of the country had followed our lead, we wouldn't have had all these problems over the years." The outrage came fast and furiously.

Lott tried his best to cling to power, offering apologies everywhere, but it wasn't enough to stem the tide. Just like in Canadian Aboriginal leader David Ahenakew's case, this was not the first time Lott had made comments about segregation. This airing, however, had been very public and even President Bush decided his comments merited serious consequences. Lott was forced to resign as Senate majority leader.

Why would a guy at the top of his game (or close to it, if he had ambitions of being president) make a comment that suggested his country would be better off if it had continued keeping African Americans segregated and denied them basic constitutional rights? Being in a gathering of good ole boys, Lott just couldn't resist the temptation to let them know he was one of them. He completely forgot that as Senate majority leader, his constituency went well beyond Mississippi's borders; he failed to consider the consequences.

It's odd that Lott felt the need to try and fit in with Thurmond, his friends, family and colleagues by saying positive things about segregation. If you look at tributes to Thurmond, they often skip over his run for president on the segregationist ticket. Jack Bass, Thurmond's biographer, believes Thurmond was embarrassed by this piece of his history. If that's true, it's certainly ironic that Lott would feel the need to bring it up.

While we're on the subject of trying to fit in, let me give you one more Canadian example. Like Scott Driemel's case, it starts with someone trying to be funny, and ends up with serious consequences.

Toronto's former mayor *Mel Lastman* probably knew very little about Mombasa, Kenya before conducting a goodwill visit there in hopes of shoring up support for his city's 2008 Olympic bid. After the mayor talked to freelance sports journalist Chris Atchison in early June, 2001, here's what the *Toronto Star* printed: "What the hell do I want to go to a place like Mombasa? Snakes scare the hell out of me. I'm scared about going there, but the wife is really nervous. I just see myself in a pot of boiling water with all these natives dancing around me."

Despite the fact this quote was buried in the sports section, condemnation came fast, moving it to the front pages of Toronto and national newspapers.

You'd think a politician trying to win the support of the hundred-plus delegates of the International Olympic Committee (IOC)-individuals who decide the Olympics' fate-would tread carefully, make it a mission not to offend. Yet Lastman's comment was perfectly designed to offend. Was he not paying close attention? Given the ballots had not yet been cast, Lastman's comments may well have contributed to the demise of the Toronto bid. During the final presentation to the IOC, Toronto's delegation was quizzed about Mr. Lastman's comments.

Tip #79 Don't make fun of "easy" targets

When I first heard about Lastman's comments, I tried to figure out why he thought he could get away with this "joke". The answer came to me quite quickly, and I think it's important food for thought. Most Canadians know very little about Africa; it is still a place that allows for wild notions and great unknowns. In other words, it's easy to pick on Africa, because who's going to complain? That reasoning may have carried logic back in the 1950s, but it just doesn't work today. Not only do people from Mombasa get newspapers and watch television; they likely heard about Lastman's comments within minutes of Toronto's media coverage via the internet.

Lastman wouldn't have made such comments about better-known, "civilized" parts of the world. The mayor made his comments while in Barcelona, Spain. What are the odds he would have made a similarly offensive "joke" about Spain? Something along the lines of, "I'm not sure about being in Spain. I'm afraid I might get my private parts stuck in someone's castanet." Or while trying to grab a few IOC votes on his way to Italy, "I'm terrified of going to Rome. I hope I don't get in the middle of a shooting match with the Italian Mafioso while eating my spaghetti." While anything is possible, it is unlikely that even Lastman would have made off-color comments to the press about an area he thought of as civilized.

There are so many parts to this faux pas. The first is his complete lack of knowledge about Mombasa and the frightening ease with which he could make a tasteless joke about it. The second is his desire to tell this to a journalist in an effort to curry favour, or to fit in with him. The third is, would the mayor have made this same joke to a Black journalist?

Many times people think they have an interested and willing audience just because someone looks like them. However, in a multicultural country like Canada, that can be a big mistake. Just because the person to whom you are speaking is not a part of the group you're "joking" about, it doesn't mean he or she wants to hear it.

A few years ago, I was taking the bus downtown to see a movie. I would normally have ridden my bike, but it was one of the few snowy days in Vancouver, and I thought I had better not risk it. After I'd walked for many blocks, a bus finally arrived. I let him know I was pleased to see him. The bus driver said, "Yeah, half of Hong Kong was stuck back there. I didn't think I'd get through." A bit stunned, I took my seat and wondered what I should do. Of course, I didn't want to get kicked off the bus, so I decided to make a comment on my way out the door. As the bus was coming to a stop, I said in a very calm voice, "About that comment..." That was as far as I got before he apologized profusely. I thanked him for his apology, got off the bus, and that was the end of it.

Clearly, this bus driver thought that just because I was a white male, I would enjoy his racist comment. Who knows, he might not have been terribly racist, but in order to "fit in" or make a joke, he thought I'd appreciate his comment; he figured he wasn't hurting anyone. (He probably thought no one else was within earshot.) Hopefully, after my comment, he realized that just because he shares the same skin colour with a passenger, doesn't mean that passenger will sympathize with or tolerate his views.

Tip #80 Staying silent doesn't help the offender

In your workplace, think about how many times people have said silly, hurtful or even outrageous things. You know people make inappropriate and questionable comments all the time, and you probably know you should do something about each one of those. How about starting by going after the outrageous ones? Think how much better your workplace or organization would be. My guess is it would be much better. It's not easy, but letting the comments pass without mention or action is doing a disservice to the people in your business and to the person making the comments. Individuals whose offensiveness is not nipped in the bud may grow into David Ahenakews or Trent Lotts, and experience a much more traumatic fall from grace later in life. I reckon it's our job to clue them in before they get to that point.

Parting Tips for Changing With The Times

Tip #81 Respond to "it was just a joke"

When teachers tell their students about bullying, they say, "teasing is when both people are having fun; taunting is when only one person is having fun." It's quite similar in the adult world, where most of us can figure out what can be taken in fun and what is a cheap shot. However, in trying to fit in, not everyone has figured out what is acceptable and what is not. When someone crosses the line and you want to take issue with something said, be prepared for "it was just a joke". With your own style, find a way to say, "not everyone was laughing".

Tip #82 "Rednecks" can surprise you

Don't be fooled by appearances. A person in your organization might look like a stereotypical "redneck" you think will balk at the first sign of inclusiveness and any idea of changing with the times. But as with all stereotypes, you don't know people until they show you who they really are. Many times I've mistakenly assumed, based on appearance, that a person is not going to easily buy into the human rights message. Then he opens his mouth and tells me about a relative who is disabled or a lesbian, and how he had to go to bat for that individual to get basic rights. Give people in your workplace a chance to accept new ideas, not based on your perceptions of them, but by their own ability to hear and accept new ideas.

Tip #83 Anonymous brown paper envelopes still work

I'm constantly told about the senior manager who hasn't changed with the times, but no one dares tell her for fear of being disciplined, ostracized or worse (usually due to past experience). If you feel that telling a boss to her face will get you in more trouble than it's worth, don't give up. There is more than one way to solve a problem. You may have the ear of your boss's peer, who can take over where you won't tread. Or, you might bring up a similar example in a meeting where your boss's light bulb will go on. Or, if all else fails, the old tried and true method of the anonymous brown paper envelope might come in handy. I don't mean you have to tattle on your boss. Instead, do your boss a favour and address the problem to her alone. You might be doing her a huge favour. I'm guessing David Ahenakew, Trent Lott or Mel Lastman all wish they had received such an envelope.

"All human beings are born free and equal in dignity and rights. They are endowed with reason and conscience and should act towards one another in a spirit of brotherhood."

United Nations Universal Declaration of Human Rights

8

Men at Work

In 1979, I worked for a school board raking rocks for the summer (don't ask) at a good wage. I got the inside scoop on the job through the retired couple from whom I rented a basement suite. Living downstairs from this couple, I quickly discerned that they were pleasant and polite. The husband, whom I'll call "Joe", was into boxing and worked for a maintenance department. Though neither of these are exactly tea-and-crumpet environments, I never, ever heard a bad word from Joe's mouth. Regardless of whether his wife was around, Joe never swore in my presence.

Then one day he came by my workplace to visit with guys he'd known for a long time, to shoot the breeze. When he caught up to my foreman we were all in the truck waiting to go out for the day. To my surprise, I discovered an alien had invaded Joe's body. Some entity began forcing him to swear: "F" this and "C" that. I learned three things that day. One, Joe holds the record for the number of swear words one can jam into a short conversation. Two, people can turn things off and on when they

> People can turn things off and on when they want to

can turn things off and on when they want to. And three, men interact differently when they are in the company of men. I discovered that in Joe's mind, at least, in order to fit in with the other guys, you've got to act like the other guys. Unfortunately for us guys, no one seems to have ever told us we don't need to act that way.

Tip #84 Don't assume guys like all the talk

When I first engaged in public speaking about workplace harassment issues, I found myself talking to all, or mostly, men, and I figured the conversations would mostly entail how male employees treat women. I was surprised to discover a different dynamic. At one particular event involving a roomful of men of all ages, once we got past the textbook learning and started talking about the need to have more respectful conversations with one another, I saw quiet nods from some of the older guys-the guys close to retirement. When I followed up with private conversations, I got the sad sense that these guys would have loved that kind of respect, but no one gave them permission to expect or demand it. They were coming to the end of their careers in a workplace characterized by toxic interactions. Since that session, I enjoy talking to men about creating a more welcoming workplace; it's a rare but welcome conversation on their part.

Don't get me wrong; sometimes male-dominated workplace training has me running to the closest bar to have a drink (or two). But there are times when we men get to connect in an unusually forthright way.

Some men consider male-dominated workplaces the greatest. To those individuals, such environments enable them to bond with one another in a way normally reserved for girlfriends, wives, sisters or mothers. They're not looking to emulate women; they are looking for more meaningful ways to interact with other men.

But there are challenges in a male-dominated workplace, and this chapter explores those and makes suggestions for dealing with them. As a supervisor of such a workplace, you can, believe it or not, ensure a respectful and productive environment without encouraging your workers to break into a chorus of *Kum Ba Yah*. Male dominated workplaces include paramilitary organizations such as firefighting and police work and in labour trades such as construction and warehouse work. Even if your workplace isn't a warehouse or a firehall, however, if some of the following trends sound all too familiar, read on.

Put-downs and insults

Let's say a bunch of guys from the firehall arrive early for their shift to catch up with the other guys and shoot the breeze. Lots of laughter and the usual banter, but two of the guys make it seem like a sparring match.

Men taking shots at one another is typical in male-dominated workplaces. Put-downs and insults are one of the most common ways men interact with one another. We have this crazy idea that when we put another man down, this builds us up. Nothing could be further from the truth, but that's how many men act, especially around other men. So what's the problem?

In a workplace setting, it's bad for employees and bad for business. Supervisors waste time defusing conflict, deciding who doesn't work well with whom, and getting men to work together as a team. It costs time and money. Most men don't have trouble with light-hearted put-downs, but when these cross the line, they rarely know how to handle it. Too often, the insults go from bad to worse on their way into the gutter. I refer to this phenomenon as the "vortex", because things spiral downward until it seems no one can escape safely.

Here are some tips for supervisors who aspire to make their workplace more respectful.

Tip #85 Decide what is respectful

Sometimes it's not easy to distinguish between good-natured ribbing and outright insults. Supervisors should go with their gut. If you think, "I wouldn't want to be on the receiving end of that," then chances are, others don't either. If gut feelings aren't your strongest point, look for clues in the way people are reacting. If one of the guys lashes back or shuts down, that's your clue something is wrong.

Tip #86 Don't worry about becoming a babysitter

You're supervising grown men who don't need constant surveillance. You need to be concerned only about behaviour and exchanges likely to cause a problem on your shift. There are many men (and women) who can get into heated exchanges about sports, politics or even religion, without causing a lasting stir. Don't ban controversy. Ban insults, over-the-top put-downs, and disrespectful language.

Tip #87 Avoid turning things formal

Save discipline for the big stuff. Simple comments such as, "Why'd you say that?" or "Would you repeat that?" can put a quick stop to disrespectful behaviour. Using discipline for simple exchanges may backfire on you. Most guys want rid of harmful comments, not the colleagues making the comments. If they think that bringing a simple problem to your attention might lead to a colleague getting disciplined, they likely won't tell you anything.

Tip #88 Watch your mouth

The guys can figure out when the supervisor is serious or not. A supervisor who says he wants more respect has to start with himself. It doesn't matter what you've done in the past; it's your job to show that people can change their ways to foster workplace harmony. When you slip up, own up and move on.

Nicknames

Nicknames are as common in male-dominated workplaces as they are in the schoolyard. In some workplace cultures, such as firefighting, nicknames are the norm and men who don't get a nickname wonder what it will take to get one. Most nicknames are a derivative of the person's name. When I was young, I used to get "green eggs and ham" and when I went to university, sometimes I'd get "hamster". No harm done. Some nicknames are earned by humourous behaviour, such as "trip" for a guy who is known to be clumsy on his feet. Unless this is caused by some disability, most guys with such a nickname laugh it off. Hence, there are plenty of examples where nicknames are considered a form of endearment or camaraderie and they are welcomed.

So where's the harm in nicknames? The harm is when guys use nicknames of characteristics we can't or shouldn't be expected to change. One fellow in a roomful of mostly male police officers told me that nicknames he used, including "Dumbo", were terms of endearment that let a fellow know he was one of the guys. Out of the corner of my eye, I saw a man flinch. I looked his way, only to see a fellow with big ears. The officer who had just spoken suddenly went on the defensive. Digging himself in deeper, he attempted to explain why he'd come up with "Dumbo", and once again, the officer known as Dumbo flinched.

> A truly insulting or disrespectful nickname causes hidden resentment, frustration and anger

As a silence in the room built, the large-eared officer spoke up to tell the group he had always hated that name, and had made that message clear all ten years he'd been subjected to it. He added that he didn't understand why people continued to use it.

Though police have the image of being big, tough guys able to take anything, this incident affirms otherwise. As I emphasize to employees who are in a tough business, if you're getting harangued by outsiders while on the job, all the more reason to be respectful to one another inside.

So, what can you do about harmful and unwanted nicknames?

Tip #89 Recognize the nickname dilemma

If an employee, especially a rookie, gets an offensive nickname, he can protest, but he knows that's usually a formula for making the name stick until retirement. He knows it's better to say nothing and pray for a better one to come along, even if the odds aren't great. As a supervisor, recognize this dilemma; don't assume silence means everything is fine.

Tip #90 Talk to the nicknamed

If you hear a nickname that makes you cringe, but the guy doesn't say anything, take him aside and ask what he thinks. Be upfront that you're just asking, and this conversation won't go anywhere unless he wants it to. Chances are with that approach, he'll tell you his true feelings about the name.

Tip #91 Don't allow "If I had to put up with it, so do you"

Instead, be a supervisor who says, "Because it was bad for me, I don't want it to be bad for you." Make a difference for those on your shift; they'll reward you with the kind of loyalty and respect money can't buy.

Tip #92 Find a way to drop the nickname

With the approval of the employee, devise a way to drop the nickname. Depending on the guys with whom you work, you can coach the nicknamed employee to deal with it himself, bring it up in a crew talk, or have a word with the most influential employee to get the guys to back off. Remember, you're doing this because hurtful nicknames cause workplace dissension. Don't let someone say it's no big deal.

Problem solving or rat?

In male-dominated and especially paramilitary environments, "ratting" on a fellow employee is an A-1 offense. Everyone is expected to handle problems on his own, or at least internally without going to the boss for support. When an internal process works effectively, issues get resolved informally, which is the best approach. However, when the process is ineffective, employees should feel comfortable getting advice or support from the boss.

I remember one guy at his wit's end. He was constantly being called names and ridiculed by a senior employee who for some reason didn't like him. He tried appeasing, then avoiding, and finally ignoring the harassing employee, but the name-calling didn't stop. He told me his wife would literally nudge him out the door in the morning saying, "Remember, the kids need to eat." He loved his work but hated his workplace.

I asked if he'd ever said anything to his supervisor. I might as well have suggested he cut off both his hands. He said he had witnessed an ostracizing that took place when another employee had gone to the boss with a problem, and he wasn't about to go in that direction. I can't say I blamed him.

But going to the supervisor shouldn't be an either/or situation: Either I talk to the boss and I'm a rat, or I don't talk to the boss and have to put up with a problem that I can't solve. Workers lacking an outlet for their problems find other outlets. On the job, they won't be productive. They will spend time thinking about their problem and ways of avoiding the harasser. Off the job, they can take out their frustration in a wide variety of ways destructive to themselves and their loved ones. Yes, even in male-dominated workplaces, supervisors need to help solve employee problems.

What can a supervisor do without turning everyone into a "rat"?

Tip #93 Try to turn "ratting" into problem solving

Get the men to trust that if they come to you, you aren't going to interfere in a manner that makes matters worse. Ensure that the guy making the complaint is involved in the issue's resolution.

Tip #94 Trusting actions, not just words

Men *will* go to someone they trust to resolve a difficult problem. But men will not necessarily trust you just because you talk about trust. Walk the talk; concentrate on real actions, and trust will follow.

Tip #95 Camaraderie should work both ways

Some male-dominated workplaces have strong camaraderie, a quality lots of men enjoy. So let your employees know that camaraderie and teamwork include protecting those being harassed or insulted. If "ratting" is a bad thing that results in someone being shunned, then talk to the guys to make harassment, abuse and unwanted insults a bad thing as well.

Men won't reveal

If you're going to get the men in your workplace to deal with insults and bad nicknames without feeling like "rats", then you've got to hear from the men. Without using beads and scented candles, you want to encourage men to find ways to express their problems in productive ways. A man struggling with a problematic personal relationship or sick child is not going to perform at full capacity. A man suffering problems with coworkers might lash out instead of trying to resolve things in a respectful way.

Men rarely express emotions or reveal much about themselves in the workplace, because revelations can be used against them like a dagger later. Sometimes it's unintentional and other times the intention is to hurt, or bring down the other fellow a notch or two. Either way, few men air their personal problems and this presents a stumbling block to supervisors aiming to solve problems.

> If men disclose a problem, it can be used like a dagger against them later.

Men tend to talk to other men about sports, interests, politics and perhaps sex (but not sexual problems). If they want to talk about feelings or problems, they'll do so with their wife (if heterosexual) or girlfriend.

"Men are driven to prove themselves-perpetually-especially to other men," explains Gail Sheehy in *Understanding Men's Passages.* Because women don't judge men in the same competitive light, a man can talk about vulnerabilities to a woman without putting himself at risk of being seen as weak amongst fellow male colleagues.

As a supervisor, how do you get men to talk about problems that affect the workplace? What *will* encourage men to share with other men?

Tip #96 Men prefer doing over talking

Men interact with other men by "doing" rather than by talking. I've known about this for years, and seen it many times in my own personal life. After my mother died, my sister would send me out on the golf course with my dad to get him to open up. He would talk while participating in one of his favourite pastimes. We could talk because we were also *doing* something. The doing might involve sports, games, or a project of some kind. So a supervisor hoping to get an employee to open up might be better off asking him to help on a work project than asking him point-blank, "How are you doing?"

Tip #97 Work with open ears and a closed mouth

Men afraid of vulnerability will go to great lengths to protect the image that they can handle anything. So if one of your employees comes to you with a problem, you need to listen, ask what he wants, and not say a word to another person unless you've been given permission. If word gets out that you opened your mouth, even with the best of intentions, your days of being a confidante are over.

Tip #98 Hold others accountable

If you hear others making fun of someone's personal problems or vulnerabilities, put a stop to it. Fostering a respectful workplace means calling people on their bad behaviour. Once you start doing this, others will follow your lead.

Fitting in

We all want to fit in. In male-dominated workplaces, even competitive ones, the idea is to not stand out too much. New employees tend to be concerned about demonstrating competence, but they're even more concerned about getting along with others and not doing anything stupid.

When I was twenty-one, I had a summer job installing business phones at a company. There, a senior employee named Don told me one day to stop my swearing. He told me I'd hardly ever cursed when we'd first met, and he thought I was trying to be "one of the guys" with my newly acquired language. He told me to be myself, that I'd be one of the guys if I did my work and proved reliable. He was dead on. I had been swearing to try to fit in with the other guys.

If colourful language were a workplace's only concern, I don't think most supervisors would have a problem with guys trying to fit in. But fitting-in attempts can cause a lot of damage. Workers Compensation has found that young, inexperienced workers are at greatest risk of being injured on the job-not just that they lack experience, but because they're trying to prove themselves, trying to fit in. Newcomers take risks that others do not. Meanwhile, ridicule and abuse (often put up with by newcomers hoping to fit in) lead to turnover, worker discontent and all-round lower productivity.

What can a supervisor do to reduce such a negative impact?

Tip #99 Don't assume employees know it all

Remember what it was like starting a new job-how many questions you had, but didn't want to ask, for fear of looking stupid. Fitting in usually means keeping quiet and observing. Supervisors need to make it clear that they and other workers expect and welcome questions from all newcomers.

Tip #100 Employees can pay dues, not sell their souls

New employees expect to pay their dues. Even those coming in at a senior level anticipate a need to learn the ropes. Harmless rituals that let someone know they have to earn their stripes are fine. However, if those rituals include harmful hazing or taking on dangerous tasks, these have to be stopped. Just because something harmful has been a "tradition," doesn't mean you should let it stand in the way of common sense. Good supervisors help workplaces change with the times.

Tip #101 Tell employees you want thinkers, not drones

Let all employees, especially new workers, know they were hired to contribute their thoughts and suggestions. That way, if they are assigned a dangerous or questionable task, they will feel comfortable speaking up, instead of dealing with the sometimes deadly consequences. We've all heard of the psychology studies that prove people will put themselves in danger as a result of not wanting to go against the crowd. Don't worry that suddenly everything you say and do will be challenged and you'll lose authority. Good employees know the boss has the authority to make final decisions, and they'll support you as long as the decisions add up to a physically and psychologically safe place to work.

Everyone has a right to a safe, supportive and harassment-free workplace, whether in the firehall, the police station, the construction site or the warehouse. Men deserve this as well.

Notes

1. Central Okanagan School District v. Renaud [1992] 2 S.C.R. 970 at p. 984.
2. Commission scolaire regionale de Chambly v. Bergevin [1994] 2 S.C.R. 525.
3. Central Okanagan School District No. 23 v. Renaud [1992] 2 S.C.R. 970.
4. Turnbull v. Famous Players Inc. [2001] O.H.R.B.I.D. No. 20, and Turnbull v. Famous Players Inc. [2003] O.H.R.T.D. No. 10.
5. Poulin v. Quintette Operating Corp. 2000 BCHRT 48, 2000 October 13.
6. Crabtree v. 671632 Ontario Ltd. (c.o.b. Econoprint (Stoney Creek)) [1996] O.H.R.B.I.D. No. 37, 1996 November 6.
7. British Columbia (Superintendent of Motor Vehicles) v. British Columbia (Council of Human Rights) [1999] 3 S.C.R. 868, December 16, 1999.
8. Pannu v. Skeena Cellulose Inc. 2000 BCHRT 56, 2000 November 20.
9. MacEachern v. St. Francis Xavier University, [1992] N.S.H.R.B.I.D. No. 2 Nova Scotia Board of Inquiry Under the Human Rights Act .
10. Harris v. Camosun College, [2000] B.C. H.R.T.D. No. 51, October 30, 2000.
11. British Columbia (Public Service Employee Relations Commission) v. British Columbia Government and Service Employees' Union (B.C.G.S.E.U.) [1999 3 S.C.R.3] 1999 September 9, p. 32-33.
12. Peebles v. Tri Spike Cedar Ltd. (c.o.b. Data Secured Limited) [1998] B.C.H.R.T.D. No. 61, F. Gordon. Oral decision: October 29, 1998.
13. Janzen v. Platy Enterprises Ltd. [1989] 1 S.C.R. 1252. 1989 May 4.
14. Jacquie Miller, "Toronto 'most racist' city in Canada Immigration report calls it 'disquieting'", *Toronto Star*, October 6, 1997, p. A1.

15. Roy James, "Black passengers targeted in Pearson searches?", *Toronto Star*, November 29, 1998.
16. *Toronto Star* series of articles on racism and Toronto Police, October 19 - 27, 2002.
17. Ontario Human Rights Commission, "Paying The Price: The Human Cost Of Racial Profiling", December 9, 2003.
18. C.N.R. v. Canada (Human Rights Commission) [1987] 1 S.C.R. 1114. SCC 1987 June 25.
19. Wright v. British Columbia Trade Development Corp.[1994] B.C.J. No. 921, British Columbia Supreme Court, February 24, 1994.
20. Ontario Workers' Compensation Appeals Tribunal, Decision No. 754/96, [1997] O.W.C.A.T.D No. 1556, December 11, 1997.
21. *CBC TV National News*, December 17, 2002.
22. *CBC TV National News*, December 16, 2002.
23. James Parker, "Contrite Ahenakew apologizes for remarks", *Saskatoon Star Phoenix*, p. A1.
24. *CBC TV National News*, December 17, 2002.
25. Darren Bernhardt, "Media draws fire from FSIN vice-chief for anti-Semitic story", *Saskatoon Star Phoenix*, December 16, 2002, p. A1.
26. R v. Ewanchuk [1998] A.J. No.150 1998 February 12, Alberta Court of Appeal, p.245.
27. Ibid. p. 250.
28. R v. Ewanchuk [1999] 1 S.C.R. 330 1999 February 25, Supreme Court of Canada, paragraph 89.
29. Ibid. paragraph 95.
30. *National Post*, February 26, 1999, p. A19.
31. Chief Justice Constance R. Glube, Chief Justice of Nova Scotia, Canadian Judicial Council, Panel Chairperson, May 21, 1999.
32. *Vancouver Sun*, November 8, 2002, p. B3.

Learn More about Managing Human Rights at Work

For more information about managing human rights at work as well as *Stephen Hammond*, his speaking, workshop and consulting services, go to his website at www.stephenhammond.ca. At the website you can:

- Fill out the **Human Rights Quiz** and find out if you and your workplace are in good shape regarding workplace human rights, or if you'll want to make important changes.
- Sign up for **frequent e-mail updates** regarding managing human rights at work. Stephen keeps his clients and interested people updated on the complex issues of human rights with his tips and suggestions.
- Read through **articles** that give brief and detailed tips to keep your business a welcoming workplace.
- View one of **Stephen's video clips,** showing him in front of an audience or being interviewed on t.v.

Buy the Book

You may purchase Managing Human Rights At Work on-line at www.stephenhammond.ca. For discounts available with volume purchases, call 604-685-8338.

Your Comments

Give Stephen Hammond your comments about this book. Or, if you have an interesting story (success, challenge or disaster) regarding human rights at work, send it to stephen@stephenhamond.ca.

Website
www.stephenhammond.ca

Speaker and Trainer

Stephen Hammond, B.A., LL.B., CSP is a member of the Canadian Association of Professional Speakers and the International Federation for Professional Speakers. In 2008 Stephen was one of only 5 Canadians to receive the designation of CSP (Certified Speaking Professional) which is the "most prestigious earned designation for platform excellence" by the International Federation. Fewer than 10% of the Federation members hold this designation.

Read what clients have to say **about Stephen** and his work, including:

- "Stephen Hammond is a gifted public speaker - one of the best." *Pat Nelson*
- "Stephen is not afraid to deliver a tough message in a respectful way." *Wendy Scott*
- "Stephen Hammond is a fabulous trainer." *Margo Gram*
- "He possesses the skills to 'get the message through' in a way that is acceptable to a demanding audience." *Tom Easterbrook*
- "We feel very lucky to have found Stephen. We wouldn't think of using anyone else." *Colleen Stanley*
- "His legal mind, sense of humour and practical point of view make great television." *Fanny Kiefer*
- "It became clear after the first presentation, that we had made the right choice." *Hans Gray*
- "Stephen Hammond is an outstanding speaker and facilitator who really connects with his audience." *Karen Pollard*

Website
www.stephenhammond.ca